The Art of Making Elegant Jewelry Boxes

The Art of Making
Elegant Jewelry
Boxes

Design & Techniques

Tony Lydgate

Sterling Publishing Co., Inc. New York
A Sterling/Chapelle Book

for Chapelle Ltd.

Owner

Jo Packham

Editor

Amanda Beth McPeck

Staff

Malissa Boatwright, Sara Casperson, Rebecca Christensen, Amber Hansen, Holly Hollingsworth, Susan Jorgensen, Susan Laws, Barbara Milburn, Pat Pearson, Leslie Ridenour, Cindy Rooks, Cindy Stoeckl, Ryanne Webster, and Nancy Whitley

Photography

Kevin Dilley for Hazen Photography

Photography Styling

Cherrie Herrick
Susan Laws
Jo Packham

Exploded Diagrams

Richard Long

The jewelry in the photographs of this book was designed and hand-made by Harriet Forman Barrett, New Paltz, New York (cast silver necklaces), Merry Lee Rae, Aptos, California (gold cloisonne enamel), Peggy and Jay Bjerkan, St. Helena, California (airbrushed ceramic jewelry), and Alison Stern, San Francisco, California (techno-moderne jewelry). Their cooperation and trust are greatly appreciated.

If you have any questions or comments or would like information on specialty products featured in this book, please contact:

Chapelle Ltd., Inc.   (801) 621-2777
PO Box 9252   (801) 621-2788 (fax)
Ogden, UT 84409

Library of Congress Cataloging-in-Publication Data Available

Lydgate, Tony.
      The art of making elegant jewelry boxes : design & techniques / Tony Lydgate
            p.   cm.
      "A Sterling/Chapelle book."
      Includes index.
      ISBN 0-8069-4287-8
      1. Wooden boxes. 2. Woodwork. I. Title.
TT200.L9397   1996
745.592--dc20   96-11988
                                                     CIP

10 9 8 7 6 5 4 3 2

Published by Sterling Publishing Company, Inc., 387 Park Avenue South, New York, N.Y. 10016
© 1996 by Chapelle Limited
Distributed in Canada by Sterling Publishing c/o Canadian Manda Group, One Atlantic Avenue, Suite 105, Toronto, Ontario, Canada M6K 3E7
Distributed in Great Britain and Europe by Cassell PLC, Wellington House, 125 Strand, London WC2R 0BB, England
Distributed in Australia by Capricorn Link (Australia) Pty Ltd., P.O. Box 6651, Baulkham Hills, Business Centre, NSW 2153, Australia
Printed and Bound in Hong Kong

Sterling ISBN 0-8069-4287-8

Contents

About
the Author

Photo by Judy Dater

My love of wood has its roots on islands in both the Pacific and Atlantic oceans. My family is originally from the Hawaiian island of Kauai, where Lydgate State Park is named after my grandfather. I grew up surrounded by the fabulous color, texture, and smell of woods such as koa, mango, milo, ohia, and sandalwood. As a young man transported to the island of Martha's Vineyard, off the Massachusetts coast, I had the good fortune to be apprenticed to a master builder engaged in restoring eighteenth-century whaling captains' homes. These were constructed by shipwrights, many without the use of nails or other metal fasteners. I was awed by what these builders' hands had accomplished, and determined to discover what mine might do.

I turned to woodworking full-time in 1978, and over the years my functional jewelry boxes and sculptural chests have appeared in art galleries, fine woodworking stores, and juried craft exhibitions throughout the country. I am a firm believer in the importance of giving away what I know, which has led to the many articles I have published on both the art and the business of woodwork. Fourth in a series of books I have written for Sterling/Chapelle, The Art of Making Elegant Jewelry Boxes has two aims: to celebrate the brilliant work of contemporary American box-makers, and to show you something about not only how, but why, people like you make beautiful things.

Introduction

It is a rare household whose members don't own jewelry, and this has made the jewelry box one of the most common accessories in every home. Because its natural, organic character harmonizes so well with the earth-sourced qualities of gold, silver, and stone, wood has always been the preferred material for jewelry boxes. Occasionally, irregular growth in wood fibers can produce gemlike flashes of figure, such as tigertail, fiddleback, birdseye, and burl. When skillfully worked, these result in boxes as beautiful, and as precious, as the jewelry they hold.

This book presents forty-one jewelry box designs by thirty-three of the country's leading box-makers. These designs invite woodworkers of all skill levels, from beginner to master, to share in the delights of creating this most useful—and most appreciated—of boxes. Thirty projects, covering everything from the simplest box for a single ring to the most intricate dovetailed chest, are accompanied by exploded diagrams and complete how-to building instructions. A Gallery section, with eleven additional boxes and chests, provides inspiration and stimulates the imagination with new design ideas. All projects are designed to be made in the home workshop, and are intended solely for personal use, and not for commercial manufacture or sale.

A basic rule for success in making jewelry boxes, as in all woodwork, is this: start where you are, with whatever tools and materials you have available. Today's woodworking magazines and tool catalogs are filled with enough fancy machinery and shiny gadgets to make any woodworker feel inadequate, and under-equipped. Remember, however, that for hundreds of years, the great masters of woodworking had no electric tools, no carbide bits, no aluminum oxide abrasives. Their masterpieces were created through elbow grease, determination, and a firm belief in the rightness of one's own way of doing things—the very attributes most home woodworkers have in abundance.

General Instructions

1. Tools

The many milling operations involved in box making can be performed in different ways, including entirely by hand, but the power tools described below will help get the job done quicker and easier.

Table Saw

The box-maker's basic tool, this machine will rip, crosscut, rabbet, resaw, dado, bevel, slot, trim, miter, and angle. A 10"-diameter blade is the most practical, and heavier-duty models are preferable because they tend to be more accurate, especially for repeated cuts. A sturdy fence, which can be used on either side of the saw blade, and an adjustable miter fence are essential accessories. Saw blades should be carbide tipped, and kept as sharp as possible. Kerf width, number, and type of teeth vary according to the particular cut to be made. Blades accumulate resin, especially when milling dense hardwoods; therefore, after each hour of use, clean them with spray-on oven cleaner.

6" x 48" Belt Sander

Sanding objects with flat surfaces is easiest on a stationary belt sander, and 6" x 48" is a convenient and widely available size. Coarse grits, such as 30x and 60x, are useful for removing large areas of excess wood and/or glue. Medium-grit belts, 120x and 150x, shape, round, and bevel, and are essential intermediate steps in the overall sanding process.

Drill Press

A drill press provides controlled drilling capability for plugs, screw holes, and invisible hinge pins. It is also useful with a sanding drum attachment, with abrasive sleeves of varying diameters and grits.

Band Saw

The band saw is essential for resawing material wider than 6", and for curved cuts.

Shaper or Router with Router Table

Many milling operations such as dadoes, round overs, and hollowing solids are best performed by either of these tools. For safe operation, as well as the wealth of applications, consult *Router Basics* and *The Router Handbook*, both by Patrick Spielman and published by Sterling.

Lathe

Some of the projects in this book, such as Judy Ditmer's Turned Gem Vessels (page 28) or Lorenzo Freccia's Half-Moon Box (page 64), require the use of a lathe. As with the router, consult *The Art of the Lathe*, also by Patrick Spielman and published by Sterling.

Joiner

The joiner is important for creating a flat face on stock, as well as for removing rough surfaces.

Thickness Sander

Although not all home shops have this tool, most mills and many cabinet shops do. It is worthwhile to gain access to, because it saves so much time in cleaning up surfaces, as well as in producing precisely dimensioned thicknesses.

* * *

No home shop, of course, has every tool, and finding ways to produce good results using only the tools and materials at hand is one of woodworking's most treasured challenges. The ingenuity bred by this challenge often leads to alternative techniques, new designs, and discoveries. In the perfectly equipped shop, where machines do all the thinking, such discoveries are rarely encountered.

Another source of innovation is the errors that even the most skilled craftsperson will inevitably make. Making a nonreversible mistake forces you to rethink, to look at the situation from a new perspective. Like making do with what tools you have, this rethinking can suggest new ideas. It is said that the mark of a true master in any field is the ability to fix whatever mistakes arise. To this it should be added that a good box-maker views a mistake not as an annoying obstacle, but rather as a creative opportunity.

2. Selecting and Preparing Stock

Much of the visual impact of the projects in this book comes from the extraordinary natural beauty of their raw material. Each project includes a listing of the woods used.

Highly figured hardwood is especially appropriate for jewelry boxes, because like pearls and many gemstones, it results from natural irregularities and deformities. Also, much of the fun of making boxes is in creating unique and unusual wood combinations, and woodworkers are encouraged to experiment with whatever is locally available. One source for interesting woods that is often overlooked is your own

An example of a highly figured wood used in a box.

backyard, and many native species that are not harvested commercially yield beautiful lumber.

Moreover, grain patterns such as burl, birdseye, crotch, curly, or fiddleback appear in these species as frequently as in more familiar woods. Neighbors, the highway department, tree trimming companies, even the local dump, can be good sources of local wood. To minimize the danger of damage to a finished box due to parts swelling or shifting, privately harvested lumber must be properly air-dried before it is used, and store-bought lumber should be kiln-dried.

Although wood in any form may be used as a starting point, the most useful dimension for box-making lumber is boards of l" or 2" thickness. Look for interesting color, grain, or figure, even if not uniformly distributed throughout the entire board.

Unlike furniture, box making does not require great quantities of lumber, and a small burl, knot, or flash of figure may be perfect for a box lid or drawer front. Use the remaining plain part of the board for drawer sides, trays, etc.

Be sure any tropical hardwoods used are purchased from a source that practices sustainable yield forest management. And be aware that despite the most careful precautions, nothing is immune to the ravages of time. Finishes dull, colors fade, woods dry out, parts shift, adhesives weaken, and cracks open and close with the passing seasons. These do not detract from the beauty of a box, but rather certify that it was made by human hands using natural materials.

Boards are often milled before they are offered for sale. A planer is used to remove the rough exterior, allowing the natural color and grain to show more clearly, and one edge is ripped straight. This assists the buyer, but also reduces available thickness, and may make it difficult to make certain parts out of a given board. Additionally, those piles of shavings on the sawmill floor are money—surfaced lumber costs more than the same lumber in the rough. For these reasons, lumber should be bought rough whenever possible to provide thicker stock to work with in the shop. Also, box-makers should develop the ability to "read" the grain of a board when still rough-sawn. This skill will per-

mit them to detect figure that a casual observer may miss.

Found in the tombs of the Egyptian Pharaohs, plywood is among the most ancient of all woodworking innovations. Many of the projects in this book use plywood in places where dimensional stability is essential, such as the bottoms of boxes, drawers, and trays. Veneer plywoods are often used in applications where the surface will be visible.

Once rough lumber for box parts has been selected and cut to rough size or "blanked out," each piece should be given as flat a face as possible, using the belt sander or joiner. Since the irregular grain of many highly figured woods leads to chipping or tear-out on the joiner, the sander is often the only realistic alternative. With one side flat, parts can be accurately ripped to thickness. Add a hair to the final dimension to allow for finish sanding, and rip on the table saw using a push stick. If the finished piece is to be greater than 3" tall, the maximum cutting height of a 10" table saw blade, two passes will be needed to complete the rip cut to thickness.

Parts are then trimmed to width, again adding a bit to the dimension to allow for edge sanding. If available, this is the time to run the parts through an abrasive planer or thickness sander. This tool offers two advantages. First, it produces parts that are uniform and precisely dimensioned, and second, it accomplishes the initial step in the sanding process, accurately laying down on the surface of the wood parallel grooves of equal depth. Parts that have been deliberately milled slightly thicker and wider are quickly brought down to precise final dimension by repeated passes through this machine. Dimensioned and sanded parts are now ready for the slots, rabbets, dadoes, or holes that will later facilitate assembly of bottoms, rails, dowels, sides, and hinge pins.

3. Milling

In box making, more than in any other type of woodworking, milling and assembly alternate in the sequence of fabrication steps leading to the final product. Dimensioned parts are glued together, and the resulting assembly is then re-milled in preparation for yet another assembly: this back-and-forth process may be repeated several times.

Each of the projects in this book includes a table of parts and their dimensions. Since the process of box making is not an exact science, however, it is important not to cut every part in a project to listed finish dimensions before beginning box assembly. When making a project with drawers, for example, you may decide to use a particularly nice piece of wood that might be thinner or thicker than the one diagrammed. As a result, the actual length of the drawer front and back may vary. Furthermore, parts with close tolerances such as lids and drawers generally have to be hand-fitted. The best approach is to make the box body first, then dimension and fabricate lids and drawers.

Finally, milling small pieces of wood can be awkward, and parts that will end up shorter than about 10" should be prepared "two up" whenever practical. Perform all dimensioning, slotting, and preassembly sanding operations on this longer, easier-to-handle stock, and crosscut to final size just prior to mitering.

The Miter Joint

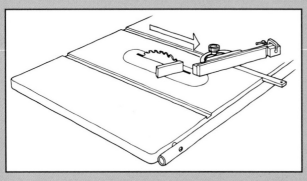

Diagram A

One of the most versatile means of joining box parts, the miter appears in many of the projects in this book. It produces a joint that is neat in appearance, does not show end grain, and can easily be reinforced with splines or slipfeathers. The secret to successful miters is accurate milling. Make sure the angles of both the table saw blade and the miter fence can be accurately set and precisely maintained. For miters on stock less than 3" wide, set the miter fence at a 45 degree angle and mill the work-piece standing on its edge (see Diagram A). For miters on wider stock, set the table saw blade at 45 degrees, return the miter fence to a right angle, and lay the workpiece on its face (see Diagram B). In either case, make trial cuts on scrap pieces first, to be sure miter settings are as accurate as available tools will permit.

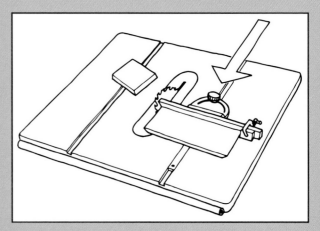

Diagram B

Slipfeathers

The slipfeathers used in several of the projects in this book (Mark Rehmar, Walnut Chest, page 102; T. Breeze VerDant, Magnolia Marquetry Box, page 85) are triangular wedges glued into saw kerfs milled horizontally in the corners of a box, lid, or other part. Slipfeathers serve to mechanically reinforce the adhesive bond in a joint, and also provide a strong visual element. They are made by passing a part or assembly over the table saw blade on a carrier block. The workpiece sits on edge in a 90 degree V-groove cut into this block (see Diagram C on facing page). (In its simplest form, a slipfeather block can be made from a 12" length of two-by-four.) The number, depth, and placement of slipfeathers vary with the design, and their thickness is determined by the kerf width.

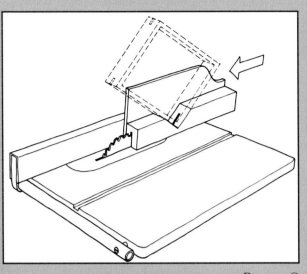

Diagram C

Trays and Dividers

A velvet-lined tray is an important feature of many jewelry box designs, and the projects in this book offer a number of different approaches. An elegant but practical version, adaptable to a wide variety of sizes and shapes, is shown in Diagram D.

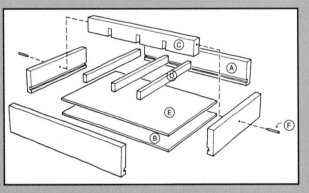

Diagram D

Stock for sides (Part A) is given a shallow saw kerf dado to receive the tray bottom. The joints may be butted as shown, mitered, or rabbeted. Eighth-inch veneer plywood with one hardwood face (Part B) is used for the bottom. The finished tray may be divided into any number of compartments. For dividers, saw kerfs are cut into the underside of a rectangular rail (Part C) that exactly fits inside the tray. Small divider strips $1/8$" thick (Part D), their top edges rounded on the sander, are then glued into the kerfs.

After it is dry from oiling, the divider is placed in the tray atop the velvet pad (Part E). Pins (Part F) driven partway through the sides of the tray into the ends of the long rail hold the divider firmly in place. These may be countersunk, and the holes filled with small dowels and sanded flush.

Velvet Linings

A simple procedure for lining boxes and trays is to wrap material such as velvet or suede over pieces of poster board or matte board, which are cut about $1/16$" smaller than the space to be lined. (Exact dimensions of the matte board will vary with the thickness of the lining material.) Make the lining material $1/2$" wider all around than the matte board, and attach with spray adhesive. For neat corners, use a sharp blade to cut off triangular sections. Apply more adhesive, and fold down the material (see Diagram E). The completed pad should jam in place tightly enough to stay put, but not so tightly that the matte board buckles.

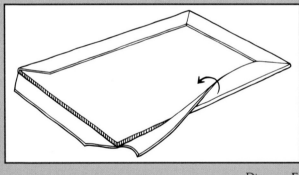

Diagram E

Assembling the Ring Holder

The boxes by Bill McDowell (Gold Chain Box, page 134, and Ring Box, page 136) and others provide a cushioned storage element specially designed for rings. This is made from rectangular pieces of $3/8$"-thick foam rubber. As shown in Diagram F (see page 12), a piece of velvet, suede, or similar lining material is wrapped over and draped between the pieces of foam. Spray adhesive can be used to bond the velvet to the foam. After assembly, this slotted

11

cushion is compressed, and held in place
between two pieces of wood.

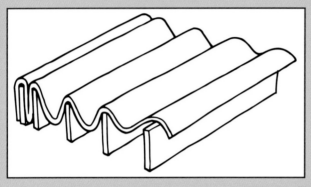

Diagram F

Slicing off the Lid

In some box designs, like those by Nan and
Bill Bolstad (Two-Drawer Chest, page 39) or
Robert Brackbill (Koa Chest, page 81), it is
important to maintain the continuity of the
grain pattern from the body of the box to the
lid. To achieve this, the box and lid are glued as
a single unit, and the lid is later separated by
ripping on the table saw. In addition to preserving continuous grain, this approach has the
advantage of eliminating the need to mill separate parts for the body and the lid, and go
through two gluing operations. One caution: in
sizing parts, remember that the saw kerf, plus fol-
low-up sanding, will consume at least $^3/_{16}''$ of
material, so dimension the four sides accordingly.

Set the blade of the table saw to a height no
more than $^1/_8''$ greater than the thickness of the
box side. After ensuring that there are no blobs
of glue or other interferences between the top of
the box and the table saw fence, rip one long
side, then each of the two short sides. Make sure
the box is held steady as it passes over the blade:
any wiggle here will require large amounts of
sanding later to restore uniform flatness to the
ripped surfaces.

Natural stresses built into the box during gluing can be released when the fourth and final
cut is made. To protect against any pinching this
might cause, insert a filler before making the
fourth cut. Use a scrap piece of $^1/_8''$ plywood or
similar material that is as wide as the cut is
deep, as shown in Diagram G. Attach the ply-

wood to a stop block; this allows the filler
assembly to rest securely on the top of the box
during the cut.

Since vibrator or pad sanders can inadvertent-
ly round-over edges, use a hand sanding block
with progressively finer grit sandpaper to clean
up surfaces after the lid has been separated.
Despite these precautionary measures, however,
it requires special care to ensure that the surfaces remain flat, especially at the corners.

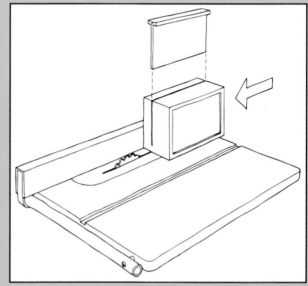

Diagram G

Laminates

Thin strips of differing woods are often laminated or glued together for decorative effect.
Since laminated parts are often resawn and
recombined with other parts, as in the lid of
Terry Evans' Inlaid Lid Box (page 77), they
must be precisely dimensioned. This means that
great care must be taken in milling the strips.
Make sure that the stock from which the strips
are cut is uniform, and that its edge is always a
perfect 90 degree angle.

Gluing up a laminate requires a "sandwich"
clamping jig, as shown in Diagram H (facing
page). Use scrap $^3/_4''$ plywood to make a base
plate (Part A) that is about 4" wider and 2"
longer than the laminate assembly (Part F). Also
make two clamping rails (Part B), each about 2"
wide, and two sandwich blocks (Part C), each

about as long as the width of the assembly. One set of clamps (Part D) glues the laminates together. A second set (Part E), keeps the assembly being glued from buckling by sandwiching it between blocks clamped on either end.

To avoid gluing the clamping blocks to the laminate—or the laminate to the base plate—line each with a single sheet of newspaper (Part G). The glue won't penetrate the newspaper, which means that when it is dry and the clamps are removed, everything should come apart easily. Any glued-on newspaper is then sanded off, along with the excess glue.

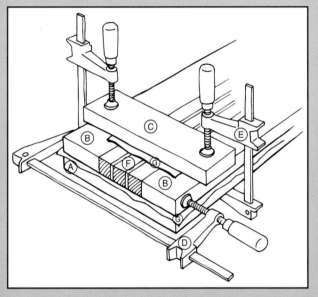

Diagram H

Invisible Pin Hinge

The lids of the jewelry box designs by Mark Rehmar (page 102) and others operate with an invisible pin hinge. This mechanism has a number of advantages: it is relatively straightforward to assemble, and requires no elaborate hardware. More important, the lid can be made separately, and when installed, it lies flush with the top edges of the box.

Parts for the lid should be dimensioned to make an exact fit with the size of the box opening. After the lid is assembled, it is fitted to the opening by sanding on edge using the 6" x 48" belt sander with a sharp fine-grit belt, such as 150x. Make sure to allow sufficient operating clearance, especially along the rear edge. The lid must then be held securely in place while pilot holes are drilled for the hinge pins.

To do this, place small strips of newspaper in the gaps between the lid and the box sides, and jam the lid in place with reasonable (but not excessive) hand pressure. Depending on the size of the gap, a thickness of four or five pieces of newspaper usually suffices. Next, mark the sides of the box for the hinge pins. Vertically, these marks should be centered relative to the thickness of the lid. If the lid is $1/2$" thick, mark them at $1/4$" down from the upper surface of the box sides. Horizontally, they are located $1/4$" plus $1/16$" from the inside face of the box back. The extra $1/16$" allows the lid, when opened, to come to rest against the box back at the desired angle (ten to fifteen degrees past vertical).

Use a drill press to drill pilot holes for the hinge pins on these marks. A brass pin or 4d or 6d finish nail works well as the hinge pin; size the drill bit accordingly. After drilling, remove the newspaper wedges, and make sure all lid surfaces are finish-sanded. Then install the lid with the hinge pins, as shown in Diagram J. The point of each pin should bite slightly into the lid, and the end should terminate about $1/8$" inside the outer face of the box sides. (If using a finish nail, remove the head with snippers.) To plug the holes and cover the end of the pins, glue in a short length of dowel of the same wood as the box, handmade on the 6" x 48" belt sander. When the glue is dry, sand off any excess length.

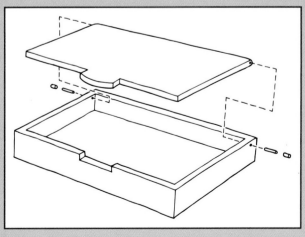

Diagram J

13

4. Sanding

The most important element in the look of a finished box is the shape and feel of its finished surfaces, and sanding is the operation that produces them. Before this point, abrasive treatments play an important role in shaping forms, and creating round overs and eased radii.

To abrade is to scratch, and abrasives such as sandpaper do literally that. Consisting of a jumble of tiny rocks glued to a paper or cloth backing, they carve into the wood a pattern of grooves, like furrows plowed into a field. When a belt sander is used, these grooves are parallel and of uniform depth. How deep is determined by the grit rating of the abrasive: as this number increases, groove depth decreases. A perfect finish is produced by repeated sanding with progressively finer grits, making these parallel grooves shallower and shallower until they become invisible.

The importance of an orderly sequence of grits cannot be overemphasized. Too broad a leap, such as going from coarse to very fine with nothing in between, will prove unsatisfactory. An attempt to remove 60x scratches with a 220x abrasive will simply produce well-sanded scratches, for the 220x rocks are too small to obliterate the grooves the 60x rocks have made. When the 60x is followed by 120x, then 180x, and then 220x, however, the result will be a smooth surface.

The flat platen of the belt sander is not useful for most curved or irregular shapes, and the best means for bringing such surfaces to the desired finish is hand or orbital sanding. Caution must be used with orbital sanders, however, as they occasionally leave circular scratches when crossing the grain, and can produce unintended round overs as the pad passes over the edge of a workpiece. Hand sanding is always the best method. The more irregular the shape, and the harder the wood, the more time and effort will be needed to achieve a good finish.

Whatever tools are used, the sanding process should be frequently interrupted to check the work with that best of all tools, the eye. A useful procedure for determining the exact condition of a surface is as follows. Hold the part in one hand and extend the arm straight. Using a window, skylight, or light bulb, make a straight line between the eyeball, the surface to be inspected, and the light source (see Diagram K).

Diagram K

Adjust the position of the hand until the angles are just right, and the light will pick up every detail of the surface, showing even the tiniest scratches. When this extended-arm inspection no longer reveals any defects, the polishing process is complete, and the piece is ready for its liquid finish.

Other Sanding Operations

In designs like those of Eric Arcese (pages 22 and 46), some box parts must be literally sculpted out of a block of solid wood. A moving abrasive belt, drum, or sleeve is often the most effective way to do this, especially if the shape is irregular or curved. Routers, carving tools, shapers, and band saws can also be used, but these leave rough surfaces that will require additional sanding prior to finish. Furthermore, any cutting tool used with figured hardwoods presents the risk of chipping and tear out.

Many boxes have flat sides that meet at crisp mitered corners. When these corners are too crisp, however, their edges are so sharp that they are uncomfortable to handle. More important, a too-sharp edge will inevitably collect tiny dings and dents, every one of which will be clearly visible. To prevent this, the sharp edges of a box should be lightly sanded, or "edge-killed," by hand prior to final finish.

In some designs, the top edges of a box are to be rounded over. The desired curve is not a true radius, but somewhere halfway between that and a 90 degree angle, and is referred to as an "eased radius." This type of edge treatment makes the finished product both more durable and more pleasing to the eye. It can be produced with a handheld orbital sander, or on the belt sander by holding the box firmly in both hands, and rocking the edge back and forth over the moving belt, grain parallel to the direction of rotation.

Where a true radius is desired, the belt sander quickly and efficiently removes the slight tool marks that even the sharpest carbide bit will leave. In many cases, there is no need to sand outside surfaces prior to assembly, especially when they are flat. Sanding after glue-up will smooth the outside surfaces, remove excess glue, grind slipfeathers or laminates flush, and correct any irregularities of rectilinearity or form, all in the same operation.

5. Assembly

For most of the boxes in this book, inside surfaces should be sanded to finish-ready condition prior to assembly, as it is usually impossible to do so afterwards.

Before starting to glue an assembly, it is always a good idea to go through a dry run, putting all the parts together first without the adhesive. This is particularly important with more complex assemblies. The dry run not only tests for fit, but also serves as a rehearsal of the assembly process, alerting the box-maker to potential problems that may arise during time-sensitive glue-up.

Another useful practice is to test every assembly for square, plumb, or true immediately after gluing, before it becomes too late to make adjustments.

Clamping

C-clamps or other screw-type mechanical clamps are essential where substantial pressure is required, as when gluing laminate strips. They are not widely used in box making, however, because the small scale of most box assemblies simply does not require that much force. What clamping does is hold the faces of a joint firmly together until the adhesive sets: for boxes, the most effective way to do this is usually with paper or cloth tape.

Adhesives

Aliphatic, or "white," glue, a convenient and economical adhesive, is appropriate for most projects. Epoxy or various types of waterproof glue can also be used. Glue should completely cover surfaces to be joined, and in general, too much glue is preferable to too little: a slight squeeze of excess is evidence that there is sufficient glue to hold the joint securely. Remember, however, that this excess will be rock hard by the next day, and difficult to remove without marring the carefully polished interior. To avoid this, let the glue dry until it reaches the consistency of stiff chewing gum. This requires an hour or so, depending on the type of glue and the temperature. The excess may now be safely removed using a sharp chisel. To prevent unwanted bonding—such as gluing the box to the worktable, or the laminate strips to the clamping jig—use a single sheet of newspaper as a liner or separator. Despite its thinness, the newspaper will not be penetrated by the glue, and when dry, everything will sand neatly off.

No matter how carefully they are made, the joints in any project may show tiny gaps or voids, which must be filled prior to final sanding. Commercial wood fillers are available, but their colors are never quite right, especially when unusual or home-grown woods are used, and a custom-made filler, or "goop," is a better alternative.

Apply a scrap piece of the wood to be matched to the belt sander and carefully collect the resulting fine dust. Mix this with glue, and force the mixture into the gaps with the flat blade of an old chisel. Experiment to determine the proper consistency. If the proportion of glue to dust is too great, the result will be runny, and when dry will appear as a glue line, which does not take a satisfactory finish. If the proportion is too little, the goop will be difficult to apply and will dry rough.

6. Finishing

Obtaining a beautiful finish has almost nothing to do with the product being used, and almost everything to do with the preparation of the surface to which it is applied. The deep, silken, liquid look of a perfect finish, with the feeling of being able to see right down into the wood, comes not from obscure ingredients or rare compounds, but from time and elbow grease. Once the right wood has been selected, all that is required to bring out the natural beauty of the wood is the proper surface preparation.

Two general types of clear finish are used in the projects in this book: penetrating oil, which soaks into the wood and then hardens, and lacquer or varnish, which lies on top of it. Unlike a dining table, a jewelry box is not designed to come in contact with water, and so varnish, with its water-resistant properties, is not needed. Lacquer's quick drying time makes it easier to work with than varnish, but lacquer is not as durable nor as water-resistant. Furthermore, its thinner nature means that more coats are needed to produce a satisfactory finish.

Penetrating oil finishes show off dramatic figure and grain patterns better than lacquer or varnish, whose multiple coats covering the surface tend to fill the pores of the wood. Oil finishes are relatively simple to apply, and have the advantage of not requiring a dust-free environment. Oil can be applied with a cloth, and rubbed in with fine steel wool. When the surface is dry, steel wool is again used to smooth it. The final step is to apply an appropriate wax, which is then rubbed to high luster by hand or with a buffing wheel.

7. Safety

Woodworking is inherently dangerous. The raw material itself can be heavy, sharp-edged, and splintery. The tools used to fabricate it are all potentially lethal. These factors, combined with noxious dust, harmful chemicals, high noise levels, and large quantities of electricity, produce an environment in which disfiguring, crippling, or even fatal injury can occur in dozens of unforeseen ways. To operate a safe woodshop, always keep this in mind.

The risk of injury can never be completely removed, but it can be reduced to an acceptable level by strict observation of certain guidelines.

• For safe operation of all tools, fully understand and adhere to the manufacturer's instructions.

• Never allow fingers to come near any moving blade or cutter. Use a push stick.

• Always wear a respirator or dust mask in the shop. Always wear ear and eye protection when using power tools.

• Always wear appropriate clothing. A heavy work apron will protect the midsection from the occasional table saw kickback. A dropped chisel hurts less on a protected toe than on a bare one—do not wear sandals in the shop.

• Never perform any operation without being satisfied that you understand it and are comfortable with it.

• Keep your mind on your work. Do not allow your attention to wander, especially when performing any repetitive operations.

• Never work when tired, in a hurry, or simply not in the mood to work. It is better to stop, or find something to do outside the shop for a while. Return refreshed and in the proper frame of mind.

Photo by Robert Debbeck

Joel Gelfand

After earning a bachelor's and a master's degree in fine arts, Joel Gelfand decided to dedicate himself to bringing art education to urban youth. He then found a job teaching sixth-, seventh-, and eighth-grade art in the South Bronx borough of New York City.

He writes, "My ten years as an art teacher taught me a lot about what it means to kids to take their own ideas seriously. Except for one kid who made it as a major-league baseball player, I never found out what became of most of my students. But I like to think that maybe some of what I taught them enriched their lives as much as the experience enriched mine.

"When it came time for me to move on to something else, woodworking seemed the obvious thing to do, since it runs in my family."

Joel's father was a woodworker, as were his grandfather and his grandfather's six brothers, and family legend has it that the tradition may go back several generations past that.

Joel has added fifteen years to that tradition so far by designing and handcrafting furniture in his New York studio, not far from the South Bronx where he once taught. His jewelry storage designs range from this delightfully simple single ring box to a complex chest (page 132), with a wooden lock and key.

Solo Ring Boxes

Photo on page 17.

This is an ideal design for a single ring, pair of earrings, or any small precious object. The woods used in the examples shown are oak, walnut, and bubinga, but the design can be made in any assortment of woods.

Because it is inadvisable to rip short lengths of wood on the table saw, start with stock 10" long, and plan to make a minimum of three boxes at a time.

• Rip two 10"-long strips of 1³/₄"-wide hardwood from a ¹³/₁₆"-thick board. Following the instructions for making a laminate on page 12, glue the two strips together separated by a ¹/₄"-thick strip of contrasting wood.
• After the glue is dry, crosscut the 10" laminate into three 3"-long blocks.
• Use a 1¹/₄"-diameter hole saw to bore a 2¹/₂"-deep hole in the center of each block.
• To make the lid filler (Part D), turn a 1¹/₄"-diameter dowel on a lathe. Crosscut a ¹/₈"-thick section off. Glue this section into the hole at the top of the lid. Alternatively, this circular lid filler part may be made from a sheet of ¹/₈"-thick stock, either on a sander, or by careful band-sawing.
• Once the lid filler is glued in place, crosscut the block to produce the body and the lid, 2¹/₄" and ⁵/₈" thick, respectively. Drill ¹/₈"-diameter holes in both for the pivot pin. On the outer surface of the lid, enlarge hole to ¹/₄" for a depth of ¹/₈".
• Mill a ¹/₈"-thick plug or pin cap (Part E), in the same fashion as Part D.
• Sand the interior surfaces smooth. Install the lid, lid pin, and pin cap. Sand and polish the six exterior surfaces of the ring box on a 6" x 48" belt sander.
• Apply an oil finish, followed by wax and buffing. Glue velvet pads into both the lid and bottom.

Part	Description	Dimensions	Quantity
A	Outer laminate	$^{13}/_{16}$" x $1^3/_4$" x 3"	2
B	Inner laminate	$^1/_4$" x $^{13}/_{16}$" x 3"	1
C	Pivot pin	$^1/_8$" x $^1/_2$"	1
D	Lid filler	$^1/_8$" x $1^1/_4$" diameter	1
E	Pivot pin cap	$^1/_8$" x $^1/_4$" diameter	1

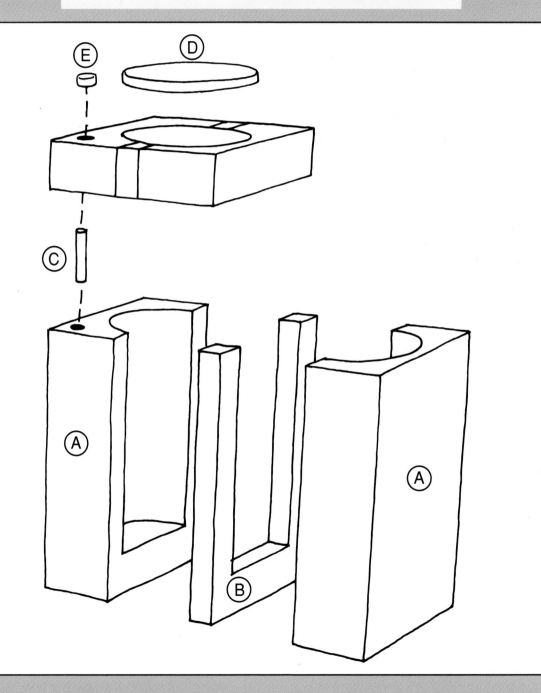

Doug Muscanell & Karen Harbaugh

Photo by Richard Abarno

Doug Muscanell began handcrafting containers from ironwood and other native species in his Colorado studio almost ten years ago, following a degree in forestry and a successful career as a project engineer for a major log home builder. "I've always loved boxes and beautiful woods," Doug writes, "and my first experiments were built from my dad's scrap pile."

"Doug is the main technician in our woodworking operation," observes Karen Harbaugh, Doug's wife. "He has more of an eye for how the natural features of a certain piece of wood expand or limit its possibilities. I have more of a mental picture of how the finished product should look. We work really well together,

Ironwood Containers

making small changes back and forth until we're both pleased with the result."

Karen was a social worker when she and Doug first met. "I was fascinated that someone could make a living doing this kind of work," she remembers. "When I first started working in the shop with Doug, I really appreciated the sense of accomplishment that I got from making something tangible. Now I do most of the finish work, which has a meditative quality I like, and I handle the people part of the business."

Karen continues, "Our dream is to collaborate on larger, one-of-a-kind pieces. There's this huge burled ironwood log we've been saving, and every time we walk by it one or the other of us has a new idea about what it could become."

Ironwood Containers

Like many slow-growing hardwoods, the trunk of the ironwood tree has a dark heartwood core surrounded by light sapwood. Doug and Karen have developed a technique for preserving the natural, organic look of the raw wood, and converting it into special containers.

• Use a log with a heavy concentration of sapwood that has been seasoned for a long time.

• Brush a section of the log free of loose debris, rotted wood, and insect residue, leaving the ribbed and pitted structure as intact as possible.

• Crosscut the thin section that will become the lid from the log.

• Using a router, hollow out the interior compartments. Sand and polish compartments until they are mirror smooth.

• Set two $1/16$"-diameter brass pins into the top surface of the box. The pins should make a precise fit with holes drilled in the lid, thus maintaining the original profile of the log when the box is closed.

Photo by Brian Schmitt

Eric Arcese

"I consider myself a traditional woodworker in that I emphasize joinery and a fine finish, but I have a nontraditional appreciation for form and shape," writes Eric Arcese. "The tops of my boxes are inspired by roadside imagery. I notice things like ski slope moguls, well-chewed pasture land, hillside cuts for superhighway exits, and topographical features like the meandering deep scallops that creeks make."

Although he is self-taught as a woodworker, Eric holds a master's degree in fine arts. After graduation, the influence of years of commuting from his rural home to school in an urban environment were reflected in his first project, "Roadside Sculpture." His sign-like constructions, incorporating optical art and galvanized materials, were installed by the side of the highway to take advantage of drive-by viewing.

Twelve years ago, he made the transition to woodworking, and set up a workshop in a rural area of New York state. As these boxes show, he has a strong preference and an intuitive feeling for the rich color and figure of natural woods.

"I started out making children's furniture, particularly toy chests and play table-and-chair sets. That led me to develop and build outdoor play structures,

in which the idea of play gets translated into what is really a large three-dimensional sculptural installation. Then one day I happened to attend a craft show—that was what led to what I'm doing today."

Single Gem Boxes

Exploded diagram on page 24.

This box for holding one treasure presents a simple but ingenious design whose sculptured lid may take an infinite number of forms. In the boxes shown, Eric has used wenge, satinwood, cherry, maple, and padouk.

• Use a hole saw or flat-bottomed drill bit to bore a 1"-deep and 1³/₄"-diameter hole in a square block of 1¹/₂"-thick hardwood. Drill two ¹/₁₆"-diameter holes to hold the lid pivot pins, as shown in the exploded diagram.

• The lid is made from a 2¹/₄"-wide laminate rod made of three layers of alternating woods. Because of the inadvisability of ripping short stock on the table saw, make the laminate rod at least 10 inches long. Crosscut the laminate rod into 2³/₈" lengths, each of which will produce one lid.

• Band-saw each length into two irregular halves. Shape the curved facets on a drum

sander using progressively finer grits.
- Attach the lid halves to the base with the pivot pins.
- Sand the four vertical sides of the box on a 6" x 48" belt sander until they are flush.
- Oil to finish. Line both the bottom and the sides of the compartment with flocking.

Part	Description	Dimensions	Quantity
A	Base	$1^{1}/_{2}$" x $2^{1}/_{4}$" x $2^{1}/_{4}$"	1
B	Lid	$1^{1}/_{8}$" x $1^{3}/_{4}$" x $2^{1}/_{2}$"	2
C	Pivot pin	$^{1}/_{16}$" x $^{3}/_{4}$"	2

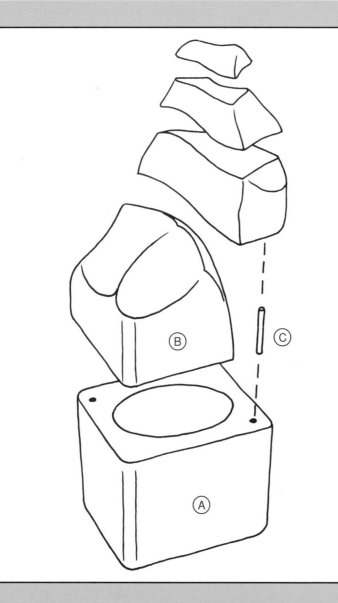

Photo by George Post

Lori Glick

years ago, at a time when you just didn't see women in the workshop. Everything was brand-new, and it was pretty scary. I cried a lot.

"Fortunately I had great friends and great teachers: a wood turning professor with the ability to make what he was doing really exciting, and a fellow student who suggested we start selling our work at local craft fairs. Now that I've gotten myself established, I can't imagine doing anything else.

"The kind of person I am doesn't leave me with much choice: I have to be creative. I feel so rewarded at the end of the day, knowing I've made something completely new, that wouldn't have come into being without me—particularly when it started out as some raggedy old board. With every box I finish, I feel like part of my soul is in it."

Half-Moon Boxes

Photo on page 25.

The delicate, feminine forms of these small containers are created using a lathe.

"My dad was in the Air Force, so when I was growing up we moved around a lot. I've always loved to create, and from as far back as I can remember, I wanted to become an artist. I've always had very strong beliefs about how I want things to look; maybe the fact that my external world changed so frequently contributed to my aesthetic sensitivity."

Lori Glick drew and painted all through elementary and high school, then studied weaving, ceramics, photography, and finally woodworking in college. "I decided that teaching art wasn't for me, so I needed a creative medium with which I could earn my own living," she recalls in her Northern California studio. "At first, I was intimidated by woodwork. This was fifteen

• Using 1"-thick stock, turn two 6¼"-diameter spheres on a lathe. Carefully hollow out each sphere until it becomes a shallow dish, with walls barely ⅛" thick.

• Rechuck the workpiece. Profile its back face to produce a 2½"-diameter raised ring. Remove from the lathe, and band-saw in half.

• Mill the hinge blocks (Part E) and the two ⅜" backs (Parts C and D) from contrasting wood. Use a 5/16" dado blade to slot the backs. Glue backs onto the box bottom and top.

• Glue the hinge blocks into the bottom, and drill pin holes.

• The half-moon inlay and detail assembly was created using a fine jigsaw and carving tools. It was then installed inside the raised ring on both the top and bottom. (Because of the angle, the drawing does not show this detail on the bottom.)

• Join the two halves of the box with the hinge pin.

• Sand the top back to follow the profile of the top.

• Oil and wax the box. Line with ultrasuede.

Part	Description	Dimensions	Quantity
A	Bottom	⅞" x 3½" x 6¼"	1
B	Top	⅞" x 3½" x 6¼"	1
C	Bottom back	⅜" x ⅞" x 6¼"	1
D	Top back	⅜" x ⅞" x 6¼"	1
E	Hinge block	5/16" x 5/16" x ¾"	2
F	Hinge pin	1/16" x 1"	4
G	Half-moon inlay	⅛" x 1" x 2¼"	2
H	Inlay detail	as req'd	1

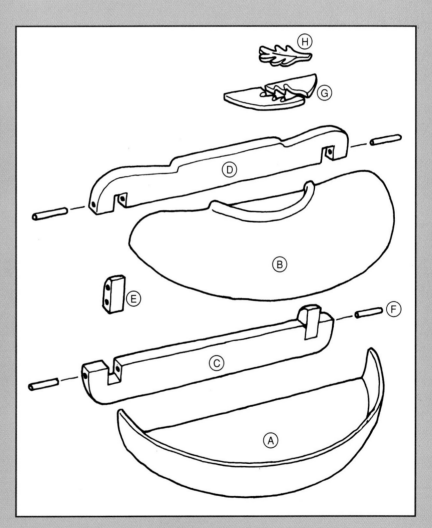

Photo by Bob Barrett

Judy Ditmer

"I knew I was an artist when I was four years old, but it took me a long time to find my medium," Judy Ditmer writes from her studio in Ohio. She is one of the country's leading wood turners, as well as the author of books on turning bowls and wooden jewelry. Judy's persistence has clearly paid off.

"As a child, I always liked to make things, and I also liked to take things apart and figure out how they work. I never got much encouragement, though, even when I went to art school, and I'd about given up on being able to do art for a living when I discovered wood turning. I happened to go to a conference on turning, and got blown out of the water. 'This is it,' I thought to myself, 'this is what I've been looking for.'

"What I like about turning is that the design process and the making process are so integrated. You don't start with a paper-and-pencil drawing, then set out to build it. Instead, you're making decisions as you do the cutting. It's a subtractive process—the result you're after is right there in the wood, waiting. When you reach that preexisting final form, there's such a sense of rightness."

Turned Gem Vessels

These delicate containers for a special piece of jewelry are constructed from parts turned on the lathe, using Macassar ebony and birch. The final shapes of the bases and handles are determined entirely by the mood of the creator; no two are ever alike.

• The larger container is 4" in diameter and $2^1/_4$" high. The smaller is $2^5/_8$" in diameter and $2^1/_2$" high.
• Turn the matching circular top and bottom sections of the box. Cut interlocking grooves on the interior edges of the two halves, so that they catch and stay together when the box is closed.
• Darken the rim of the larger box with ink.
• To make the bases and handles, start by turning a second set of parts, with the same diameter and curvature as the top and bottom. From these parts, sections of varying sizes are cut out on the band saw. Using a shaft-mounted drum sander with various diameter sleeves, shape and curve the edges, some of which will later be darkened with ink.
• Glue the base and handles to the box. Finish the entire box with spray lacquer.

Photo by George Post

His distinctive work appears in many important exhibitions and collections, and recently he was awarded a fellowship from the Washington State Arts Commission.

Box on Stilts

Exploded diagram on page 32.

For some woodworking projects, naturally occurring features of hardwoods such as knots, burls, and voids are viewed as a defect. In this design, Randy Cook has shown how the right hands can transform such apparent defects into sources of beauty and visual strength. The wood for this box could be rescued from a board whose ordinary-looking remainder could well have gone on to make the face frame of a kitchen cabinet, or drawer sides for a small chest. Randy, of course, is after the bark-encrusted void and the sparkling irregularity of the compression curl.

This box is designed to hold a single special item of jewelry, a treasure, or a gift.

Randy Cook

Although Randy Cook's academic training was in metal sculpture and ceramics, his father's woodshop gave him a feel for woodwork from an early age. "My family valued the arts," he remembers. "My grandmother made ceramics, and my great-aunt was a painter, so there was quite a tradition. Although I learned a great deal in my high school and college art courses, none of it really sunk in till I won an Archie Bray fellowship in clay. And now that I work in wood, some people still say my boxes look like wooden pots."

Randy was drawn to wood as a medium, he says, "because there's always a chance to repair it. Once you put a clay pot into the kiln, you lose control; you never know what it's going to look like when it comes out." His fascination with the knots, voids, and irregularities that give his "boxes on stilts" their distinctive look came from hating the fact that such pieces of wood usually went into the wood stove. "It really irritated me to see all that beautiful material get thrown on the fire, so I found a way to show it off."

As a ceramic artist, teacher, and now a woodworker, Randy has earned a national reputation.

• Begin with two pieces of $3/4$"-thick highly figured maple, each about 8" wide and a little greater than 8" long.
• To produce the four sides, band-saw each piece of maple in half. Sand smooth with an abrasive planer.
• On the inside face of each side, rip a saw kerf dado $1^1/8$" down from the top edge to hold the compartment bottom. Miter the sides.
• Assemble the box, with the bottom in place.

• Shape the legs or stilts from ⅛"-thick rosewood. Glue in place with ⅛" maple dowels whose ends are left projecting ⅛".

• Ebonized walnut was used to make the lid, to which Randy attached his characteristic handle. The handle was carved from rosewood, then wrapped with a thin strip of bamboo, and set atop a ³/₁₆"-thick brass plate, ½" x ¾".

• Line the compartment with a velvet-wrapped pad (see page 11).

Part	Description	Dimensions	Quantity
A	Side	¼" x 4" x 8"	4
B	Stilt	⅛" x ⅝" x 7¼"	2
C	Stilt pins	⅛" x ⅜"	4
D	Compartment bottom	⅛" x 3¾" x 3¾"	1
E	Lid	½" x 4½" x 4½"	1
F	Handle	½" x ¾" x 2½"	1

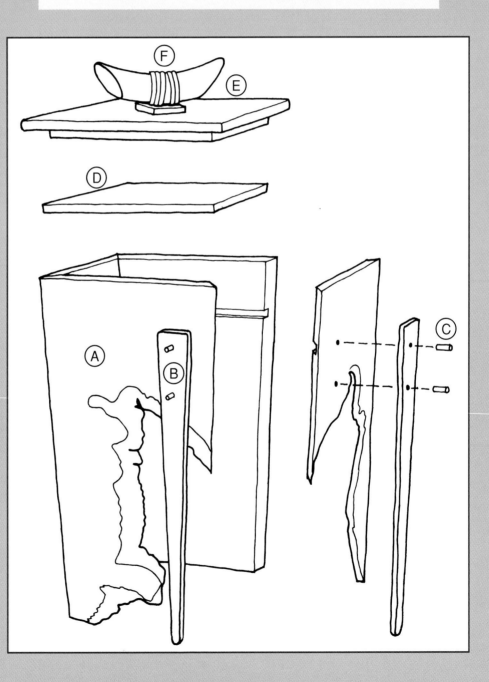

John Russell

Photo by Bob Barrett

"My father was a movie and television director in Los Angeles," John writes, "and he made the huge mistake of putting me in one of his movies when I was six. I loved it, and wanted to keep on acting, but unfortunately (or perhaps fortunately) my parents refused to let me do any more until I was old enough to 'handle myself.'"

After graduating from UCLA as a graphic design major, John joined the Army and served in the Vietnam War as a second lieutenant. When he left the Army, he went straight to New York to resume his acting career. "I worked in Broadway and off-Broadway shows, regional theater, and television, but after years as a professional, the thrill just wasn't there for me anymore.

"One day a piece of wood marquetry in an antique store caught my eye," he continues. "That led me to

Multi-Part Cross Box

experiment with small pieces of veneer, which I could take with me and work on between performances while on tour. I began making simple boxes as gifts for family and friends, and realized that finally, thirty years after graduating, I was using my graphic design training."

John remarks, "Although I'm still pretty new at this, I get ideas and encouraging feedback from my customers. I view my work as painting with wood, and the incredible range of available colors makes this one of the most rewarding things I have ever done."

Multi-Part Cross Box

Photo on page 33.

In this unusually shaped box, John Russell's primary focus is on the veneer design of the surface, so he has deliberately kept the construction details as straightforward as possible.

Although special tools and techniques are required for applying traditional furniture veneer, many veneer supply companies also offer the thinner, easier-to-handle material that was used on this box. Easily cut with a straightedge and sharp utility knife, these come on cloth or paper backing, some with peel-off adhesive, and an enormous variety of species are represented.

The veneers used are English brown oak, Macassar ebony, and tigerwood.

• The bodies of the central cross-shaped structure and the four corner boxes are all made from 1/4" pine. Glue together using simple butt joints.
• Glue squares of 1/8"-thick plywood across the entire dimension to serve as lid liners and bottoms. Because the exterior surfaces will be veneered, the seams will not be visible.
• Glue and veneer the body and lid of each segment as a single unit. Slice apart.
• Thin sheets of pine inside each box serve to hold the lid snugly in place. Line with ultrasuede. Finish box with spray lacquer.

Photo by Stefani Photography

Bill began his career as an industrial arts teacher in Minnesota, and Nan, also a Minnesotan, has a degree in English. Together, over the past twenty years, they have integrated their lives, their children, and their work in a way that is only possible for the self-employed. "That's the most important aspect of our business," Bill observes, "Nan and I being able to work together and to be around our kids as they grow up. We're grateful for the opportunities we've had that often aren't available to people with conventional jobs."

Ring & Necklace Box

Photo on page 35. Exploded diagram on page 38.

This ring and necklace box is made from maple. Both the box and its door utilize a dado joint, which features a $1/4$"-thick projection, or tenon, that fits into

Nan & Bill Bolstad

In 1974, Nan and Bill Bolstad began Wooden Nickel Woodworks, selling their jewelry boxes and other wooden handcrafts to the public and to fine woodworking galleries throughout the country. Their business was so successful that four years later they left their midwestern roots and moved to rural Oregon.

Nan and Bill have become famous because of their rare ability to create designs with the perfect marriage of form and function. The sophisticated shapes of their jewelry boxes are meticulously handcrafted from the finest hardwoods, yet when opened, each is a marvel of functionality. Years of carefully listening to what people want in a jewelry box enabled the Bolstads to respond with boxes that incorporate all the most useful storage features.

a corresponding $1/8$"-deep slot. *This joint has three advantages: it is extremely strong and durable, it can be milled using conventional tools, and it provides an interesting visual detail.*

This box uses a type of hinge that eliminates the need for chiseling mortises and struggling with tiny, soft brass screws.

• Mill both the male and female ends of the dado joint, using either a dado blade or a standard carbide-tipped saw blade.

• Make the back of the box from $1/4$" maple veneer plywood. Dado into each of the four sides for added strength.

• The door panel is made of Western maple burl, rounded and shaped.

• For the hinge, mill two skinny slots into which $1/32$"-thick leaves will be jam-fitted.

• Use brass hooks for chains and necklaces, and a magnet catch to hold the door securely shut.

• Line the interiors of both the door and the body with velvet wrapped around a thin cardboard blank (see page 11).

• Make the wooden parts of the ring tray with a half-lap joint, as shown in the exploded diagram. Before installing the tray, attach the box to the base with two #6 x 1" wood screws. Glue tray in place.

• Make the interior of the tray using five pieces of cardboard wrapped with velvet. These will produce four slots for ring storage (see page 11).

Part	Description	Dimensions	Quantity
A	Base	$3/4$" x 5" x 9"	1
B	Door panel	$1/2$" x 6" x 11"	1
C	Door side	$1/2$" x $1^1/4$" x $12^1/4$"	2
D	Door top/bottom	$1/2$" x $1^1/4$" x $6^1/4$"	2
E	Back	$1/4$" x $6^1/4$" x $11^1/2$"	1
F	Side	$1/2$" x $2^7/8$" x $12^1/4$"	2
G	Top/bottom	$1/2$" x $2^7/8$" x $6^1/4$"	2
H	Hinge	n/a	2
J	Necklace bar	$5/8$" x $1^1/8$" x 6"	1
K	Necklace bar screw	#6 x $1/2$"	1
KK	Necklace hooks on bar	n/a	6
L	Ring tray front/back	$1/4$" x $1^1/4$" x 6"	2
M	Ring tray side	$1/4$" x $1^1/4$" x $2^1/4$"	2
N	Ring holder insert	1" x $5^1/2$"	as req'd
O	Magnet catch	n/a	1
P	Necklace hooks on inside of door (not shown in drawing)	n/a	21
Q	Attachment screws (not drawn)	#6 x 1"	2

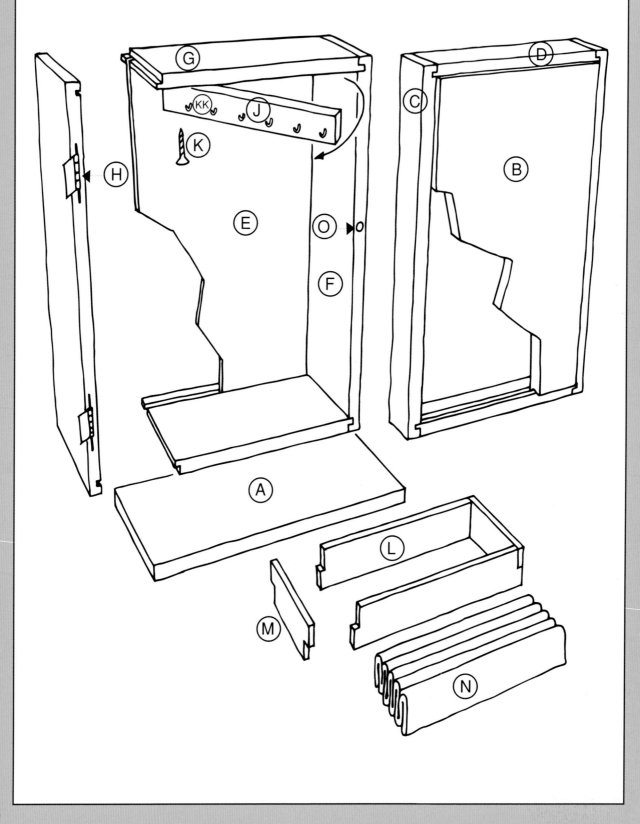

Nan & Bill Bolstad

Biography on page 36.

Two-Drawer Chest

Photos on pages 39 and 42.

This compact design combines the easy access of a hinged lid with the storage capacity of drawers. Most important, the Bolstads have incorporated one of the most practical systems for ring, necklace, and chain storage ever designed.

Walnut and Western maple were used in this chest, both with high figure and rich grain patterns.

• Parts are connected using a dado joint. The box is glued up as a single unit, and the top is later ripped on a table saw.

• Mill the dadoes for the bottom, compartment bottom, and drawer guides in the sides. Remove a section of their front edge below the attachment point of Part FF (compartment front).

• Hold the lid panel in place by a keel that fits into a ¹/₈" saw kerf dado (not shown in the drawing). Finish-sand panel, and round its upper edges prior to assembly.

• To assemble, glue up the body with sides, back, both bottoms, lid panel, and compartment front. Remove the lid section by careful ripping on the table saw. To preserve the original grain pattern, all the parts that make up the front of the box are taken from a single board.

• Glue in the bottom trim rail and the drawer guides. Mill the dadoes in the drawer sides (which capture the guides) with a router or table saw dado blade. Assemble drawers. Give all the exposed edges an eased radius by hand or with an orbital sander.

• The lid and compartment of this box contain fittings specifically designed for rings, necklaces, and chains. A ring cushion goes in the 1"-wide space between Part R (compartment dividers). To make ring cushion, wrap two pieces of ¹/₄" x ³/₄" x 11" foam rubber with the same velvet used to line the compartment and drawers. Place between the two pieces of wood to form a tight fit with just enough give to securely hold up to a dozen rings.

• Attach eight brass hooks for

Part	Description	Dimensions	Quantity
A	Side	¹/₂" x 6³/₈" x 6³/₈"	2
B	Back	¹/₂" x 6³/₈" x 12¹/₈"	1
C	Bottom	¹/₄" x 6³/₈" x 11¹/₂"	1
D	Compartment bottom	¹/₄" x 6³/₈" x 11¹/₂"	1
E	Bottom trim rail	⁷/₁₆" x ¹/₂" x 12¹/₈"	1
F	Drawer guide	¹/₄" x ⁵/₁₆" x 6"	4
FF	Compartment front	¹/₂" x 1¹/₂" x 12¹/₈"	1
G	Lid side	¹/₂" x 1¹/₄" x 6³/₈"	2
H	Lid front/back	¹/₂" x 1¹/₄" x 12¹/₈"	2
J	Lid panel	⁵/₈" x 6³/₈" x 11¹/₂"	1
K	Leaf hinge	1¹/₈"	2
L	Top drawer front	¹/₂" x 1³/₄" x 12¹/₈"	1
L	Bottom drawer front	¹/₂" x 2¹/₂" x 12¹/₈"	1
M	Top drawer body front/back	¹/₂" x 1⁵/₈" x 10³/₈"	2
M	Bottom drawer body front/back	¹/₂" x 2¹/₈" x 10³/₈"	2
N	Top drawer body side	¹/₂" x 1⁵/₈" x 6"	2
N	Bottom drawer body side	¹/₂" x 2¹/₈" x 6"	2
O	Drawer bottom	¹/₄" x 5⁵/₈" x 10⁵/₈"	2
P	Attachment screw	#6 x ³/₄"	4
Q	Compartment divider	¹/₄" x 1³/₈" x 6"	2
R	Compartment divider	¹/₄" x ⁷/₈" x 11"	2
S	Lid support	As req'd	1

necklaces or chains across the inside of the lid itself. Once attached, the remainder of their length rests comfortably in a fabric pouch with an elastic upper edge.

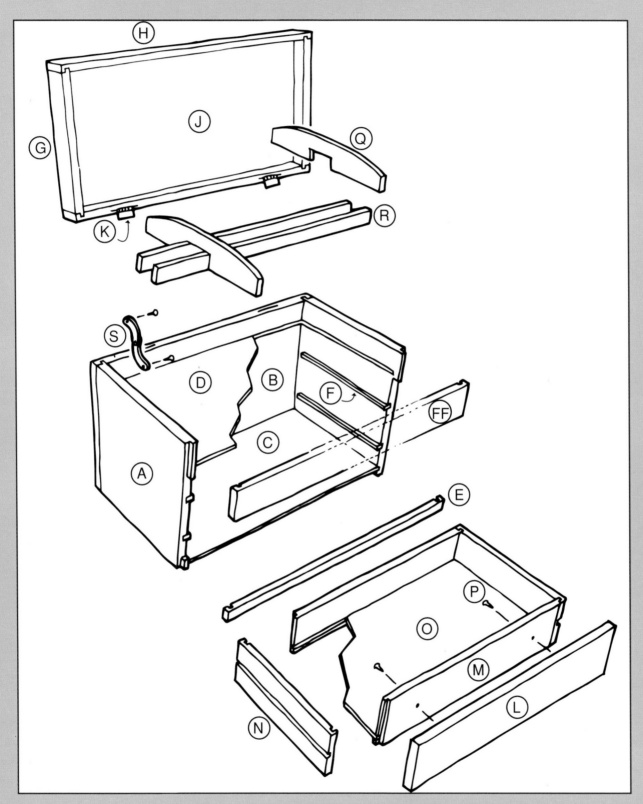

Dan Secor

It is often said that the classic beauty of Dan Secor's work derives from his strong sense of composition, color, and design. Some of this he absorbed while growing up—both of his parents worked in the arts—and some he gleaned from his years as a jeweler's apprentice. Everything he did, from observing the master set a precious gem, to inlaying belt buckles with colorful wood and bits of silver wire, made an imprint on his aesthetic consciousness.

"Ever since I started making boxes, I've been a one-man shop. I'm flattered that my work has won so many awards, and has been featured at so many fine galleries and craft exhibitions, but I'm resisting the pressure to expand. Of course, my designs may evolve and change. But I'm committed to maintaining what I consider the most important thing—I want to make heirloom-quality work, the kind of work that

Photo by Richard L. Faller

Deco Cross Box

43

becomes a family treasure, passed on to children and grandchildren."

Although his small New Mexico shop contains the basic woodworking tools, much of the detailing of Dan's boxes is done by hand. "I'm fortunate to have my workshop in my home, and be married to a woman who is herself an artist. What's more, when it's time for me to take a break, we're surrounded by these marvellous hills. Nothing refreshes me more than taking a long walk through this beautiful country with my son."

Deco Cross Box

Photo on page 43.

Unlike traditional marquetry, with its flat surfaces, Dan's lid inlay design features multiple horizontal planes, which give its classic design a subtle sculptural quality. The four rectangular maple panels are set slightly lower than the figured mahogany border. Likewise, the ebony insets in the four corners and in the central diamond are also slightly higher or lower than their surroundings.

• Glue this box up as a single unit (the lid is later ripped on a table saw). The sides are milled 4" wide, which allows enough room for side, lid, saw kerf, and sanding.
• Mill a saw kerf slot for Part E (tray rails) into the front and back.
• Part H (lid liner) forms a base to hold the lid inlay and provides stability for the box body during glue-up.
• Use a round-over router bit to radius the outer edges of box and lid.
• Miter the tray. Give the large tray divider a curved profile and a three-hole central detail. Drill mortises for the 1" oblong invisible hinge. Chisel following manufacturer's instructions.

To enhance the symmetrical effect of the lid, Dan has sliced a single block of maple into four ⅛" sections, each a near mirror image, which are laid out in bookmatch fashion. The edge banding is created from a variety of woods. Prior to assembly, each piece is carefully rounded. A tiny gap is left between the many elements as they are glued into place, to allow for potential expansion and contraction of the wood.

Part	Description	Dimensions	Quantity
A	Front/back	$3/4"$ x 3" x $13^1/2"$	2
B	Side	$3/4"$ x 3" x $8^1/2"$	2
C	Side liner	$3/16"$ x $2^1/4"$ x 7"	2
D	Bottom	$1/8"$ x $7^3/4"$ x $12^3/4"$	1
E	Tray rail	$1/8"$ x $1/2"$ x $11^5/8"$	2
F	Lid front/back	$3/4"$ x 1" x $13^1/2"$	2
G	Lid side	$3/4"$ x 1" x $8^1/2"$	2
H	Lid inside liner	$1/8"$ x $7^3/4"$ x $12^3/4"$	1
J	Lid inlay	$1/4"$ x 7" x 12"	1
K	Tray front/back	$5/16"$ x $1^1/8"$ x $11^1/2"$	2
L	Tray side	$5/16"$ x $1^1/8"$ x 7"	2
M	Tray bottom	$1/8"$ x $6^5/8"$ x $11^1/8"$	1
N	Tray divider	$5/16"$ x $1^1/8"$ x $10^7/8"$	1
O	Tray divider	$1/8"$ x $5/8"$ x $6^1/4"$	4
P	Hinge	1"	2

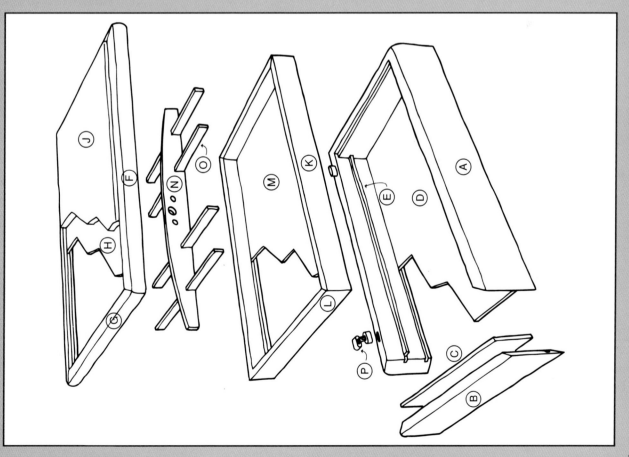

Eric Arcese

Biography on page 23.

Sculpted Box

Photo on page 48.

This playful, brightly colored design is as much a delight to open as it is to behold: each of the irregularly shaped parts of the top swings out on a brass pin. Since the parts must be opened and closed in a certain order, Eric's design is like a puzzle box as well.

Sculpted Box

- Make the body of the box from a laminate which consists of four $1/2$"-wide pieces of wood, each 32" long. The woods and thicknesses used in the model are padouk, $5/16$"; maple, $7/16$"; wenge, $5/8$"; and padouk, $7/8$".
- Clean up the laminate on a table saw or abrasive planer. Crosscut it to appropriate length for the four sides.
- Mill the overlap joints, with their reinforcing tenons.
- Use a $1/4$" dado blade to mill the three slots in which Part J (short dividers) will sit.
- Make the dado for the $1/8$" plywood bottom using the width of the table saw kerf.

- Sand the insides of the four sides.
- Glue up the box.
- Make the lid of the same woods as the box. The order and thickness follows the same pattern as the box. Use 6" x 10" stock when gluing up the lid.
- When lid is dry, band-saw into four sections. Give each section a sculpted profile using a drum sander. The resulting shapes will appear to distort the straight lines of the lamination.
- Drill parts D and G (two largest lid blocks). Pin these parts to the box so that they swing out from the left rear and right front corners, respectively.
- Parts F and E (smaller blocks) can only be opened after the larger lid blocks are moved.
- Oil and buff box. Line the bottom of the box with velvet. Insert the dividers into place.

Part	Description	Dimensions	Quantity
A	Front/back	$\frac{1}{2}$" x $2\frac{1}{4}$" x $9\frac{3}{4}$"	2
B	Side	$\frac{1}{2}$" x $2\frac{1}{4}$" x $5\frac{3}{4}$"	2
C	Bottom	$\frac{1}{8}$" x 5" x 9"	1
D-G	Lid section	$2\frac{1}{4}$" thick, as req'd	4
H	Lid pivot pin	$\frac{1}{16}$" x $1\frac{1}{2}$"	4
J	Divider	$\frac{1}{4}$" x $1\frac{1}{2}$" x $5\frac{1}{8}$"	3
K	Divider	$\frac{1}{4}$" x $1\frac{1}{2}$" x $8\frac{3}{4}$"	1

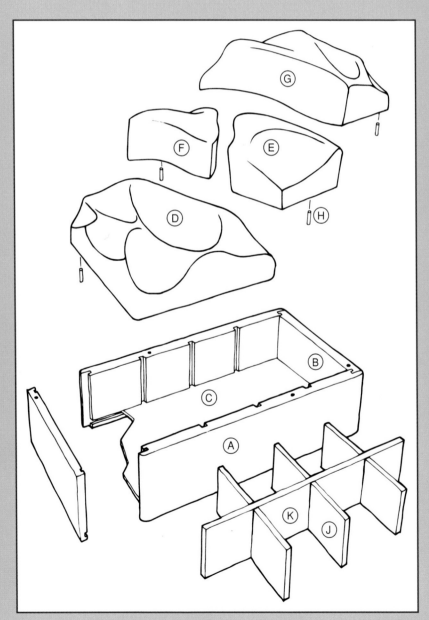

Peter Bull

Timber framer, furniture builder, and box-maker extraordinaire, Peter Bull exemplifies the new breed of designer craftsman. His remarkable technical abilities are used to celebrate the natural qualities of the woods he loves—not to dominate them. Every piece his hands create illustrates his commitment to the belief that good design is ultimately—and fundamentally—personal.

After graduating from Ohio State, Peter went on to develop both his aesthetic sense and his technical skills at leading craft schools. He writes, "The experience that most educated my eye was a series of college courses I took on photography. Although I'm interested in furniture as well as architectural interiors, I like boxes for their secret quality—plus they're very personal to people."

Nestled among holly, sycamore, sourwood, and Bradford pear, his Georgia studio is a long way from

Legged Box

49

the little village in England where he lived until, when he was four, his family emigrated to America. "The character of my surroundings has always been a powerful source of inspiration for me," Peter remembers. "North Georgia is one of the most beautiful places on earth, and I know that my work is energized by the connection I feel to this marvellous countryside."

Legged Box

Photos on page 49 and page 52.

The subtle detailing and contrasting woods Peter Bull uses in this box give it an air of delicacy despite its size. Made of wenge, the box itself is of mitered construction.

- Mill a dado for the 1/4"-thick plywood bottom of the box for added strength. Mill a 1/4" dado on the inside face of the front and back, starting 1³/4" up from the bottom edge. This dado will later be filled by Part J (tray rail).
- Make the lid panel by gluing together two pieces of ³/8"-thick quilted maple on edge.
- Mill a 1/8" long by 1/4" deep rabbet in the box sides, to set lid panel in prior to glue-up. The top surface of the panel will be about 1/8" higher than the top of the box sides.
- After the box is glued up, mill a 5/8"-long slot (1¹/8" deep) into each of the four corners, starting at a point 1/2" up from the bottom. This slot will later be filled by Part M (leg cap), which also acts as a

reinforcement for the corner joint.
- Carefully separate the lid by cutting it around the perimeter on a table saw (see page 12). The sides should be 4" high at the time the box is glued together to allow for the width of this saw cut, as well as sanding the surfaces smooth.
- Give the four sides of both box and lid a slight angle by moving the table saw fence to the left of the blade, angling the blade 8 degrees, and carefully shaving off a small amount of material.
- When completed, the box will measure about 11¹/4" x

18⁵/8" at the bottom, but only about 10³/4" x 18¹/8" at the top.
- Part K of the three-part leg assembly is an angled block of tiger maple. It has a 5/16" dado along its vertical edge into which Part L (wenge ornament) will be glued. Part K forms an interior right angle. Glue upper portion of Part K snugly against the exterior right angle of each box corner.
- Glue the triangular leg cap, with its beveled edge, into the horizontal slot, and onto the leg. Both the leg caps and the handle of the box are made of spalted maple, which produces

Part	Description	Dimensions	Quantity
A	Lid side	⁷/8" x 1¹/8" x 11¹/4"	2
B	Lid front/back	⁷/8" x 1¹/8" x 18¹/2"	2
C	Lid top	³/8" x 4⁷/8" x 17¹/4"	2
D	Lid handle	⁵/8" x 1⁵/8" x 2"	1
E	Handle pins	¹/8" x ¹/2"	2
F	Front/back	⁷/8" x 2³/4" x 18¹/2"	2
G	Side	⁷/8" x 2³/4" x 11¹/4"	2
H	Bottom	¹/4" x 10¹/2" x 17³/4"	1
J	Tray rail	¹/4" x ¹/2" x 16⁷/8"	2
K	Leg	1¹/2" x 1³/4" x 3"	4
L	Leg ornament	⁵/16" x ¹/2" x 3"	4
M	Leg cap	⁵/8" x 3" x 3"	4
N	Brass hinge	1" x 1¹/4"	2
O	Tray front/back	³/8" x 1" x 8³/4"	2
P	Tray side	³/8" x 1" x 9¹/2"	2
Q	Tray bottom	¹/8" x 8³/8" x 9¹/8"	1
R	Tray slipfeathers	¹/4" x ¹/2" x ¹/2"	4
S	Tray dividers	¹/4" x ⁵/8" x 8"; 8³/4"	7
T	Bottom divider	¹/4" x 1" x 9¹/2"	3
U	Bottom divider	³/8" x ¹/2" x 16⁷/8"	2

the striking pattern of irregular black lines.

• Make the sliding interior tray just like the box itself with mitered corners, reinforcing horizontal slipfeathers, and a slight angle, so that the dimensions of the tray are a little greater at the bottom than at the top. Line the sliding interior tray with a soft fuzzy fabric.

• Make compartments for various types of jewelry with a system of dividers inside the tray as well as below it.

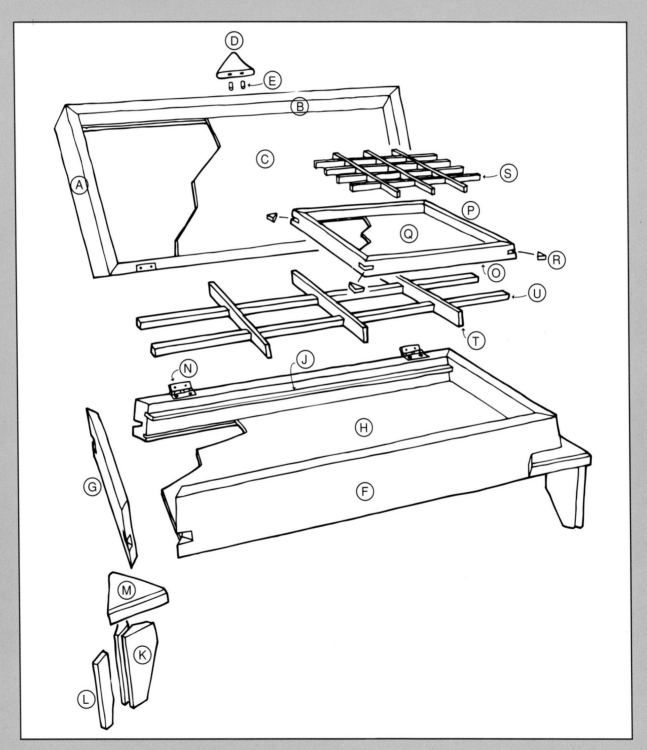

Bristlecone Pine Box

Photo on page 53.

More than a century ago, a naturally occurring fire burned through a forest of bristlecone pine trees high in the San Juan mountains of Southern Colorado. Although the fire caused many of the trees to die, some are still standing today, their once blackened faces weathered by wind and countless storms to a beautiful silver/gray patina. Much of this wood has been harvested for firewood, but to the Brimhalls, it is the raw material for this drawered band-sawn chest, which stands 11" high, 11" deep, and 13" wide.

The Brimhalls have perfected a technique for creating delightful curved compartments within their drawers, some of which include small sliding trays.

- Band-saw a ½"-thick section off the rear face of the log, at a right angle to the grain.
- Using a drill press and jigsaw, saw out the six drawers from the body.
- Glue the rear section back on.
- The drawers are made from long plug-like shapes. Cut a ½" section off the front and back ends.
- Remove the interior of the drawer with a band-saw cut. Glue the ends back on.
- Use a 6" x 48" belt sander to sculpt and polish the fronts of the drawers, including subtle spaces for finger access.
- Carefully oil and wax the raw wood. Leave intact the contrast between two strikingly different states: the ancient, naturally weathered, and the new, artfully sculpted.
- Place round felt pads inside the drawer cavities to ensure a snug fit. Line all drawers with purple velvet.

Photo by Summit Photo

Paul & Cinda Brimhall

"Except for a few years in Utah and California, we've lived all our lives in Colorado," writes Cinda Brimhall. "Simplicity and self-sufficiency are important to us, and the old fence posts and bristlecone pine we use to make our boxes are very much a part of the landscape where we live."

With farmers and ranchers for parents and grandparents, the Brimhalls are at home on the land. Unlike most box-makers, they don't have to drive to the lumberyard for wood. Cinda explains, "For fence posts, most of the old ranches used Rocky Mountain juniper, which doesn't like to grow much below 7,000 feet elevation. After it's been cut into fence post length and stood in the ground for a hundred years, wood like that develops character. The bristlecone pine is the same way: since the forest was burned over in the 1880s, it's just been standing there.

"Our work is about the rugged beauty of nature, and the passage of time in what used to be the Old West. Useful objects like our drawered band-sawn chests can go anywhere, and when they do, they carry with them the strength of the land that bred them, as well as its integrity and spirit."

Photo by David Palnick

"I'm experiencing a tremendous learning curve right now. I want to take mixed media further than I have, so I'm enrolled in a metalsmith class. The possibilities for combining other materials with wood fascinate me, and I want to use metal and stone to move in a more sculptural direction. For the foreseeable future, it's an ongoing educational process."

Mixed-Media Box

Photo on page 59. Exploded diagram on page 58.

For the lids of this architectural design, David has used a light gray, pepper-and-salt sheet plastic material often used for kitchen counters. This material is available from a number of manufacturers in a wide variety of colors, patterns, and dimensions. Most can be milled and sanded using woodworking tools, however, read and follow manufacturer's instructions for whichever material you select. A 4"-diameter mirror was glued to the inside of the top compartment lid.

- Crosscut a 24" length of 1"-diameter walnut dowel into the lengths listed on page 58. These are the legs.
- Make the three containers from 7" lengths of 1³/₄"-thick mahogany, each 5" wide. Mark where the legs will be located on each container, and drill 1"-diameter holes at marks.
- Band-saw the curved triangular shape of the containers. After band-sawing, the remaining portions of the holes will make a snug fit for each leg.
- Smooth out any band saw marks on the exterior of the container with a 6" x 48" stationary belt sander.
- Hollow out container interiors using a 4"-diameter hole saw. Clean up edges using a small sanding drum attached to a drill press.
- Connect the legs to the containers with ¹/₄" dowels located at the vertical center of the containers. Mark and drill into the side of each container, making sure not to drill completely through the thin wall. Mark and drill corresponding holes in the legs.
- Sand to finish and to remove any sharp edges.
- Assemble box using small amounts of glue.
- Make lids as desired (see above).
- Oil-finish. Line compartments with felt.

David Palnick

After twenty years working as a computer professional, in 1994 David Palnick decided to upgrade woodworking from a hobby to a full-time occupation. "My dad was a cabinetmaker, and his hobby was making violins," David recalls. "As a kid, I spent a lot of time in his basement shop, and I think I kind of learned from him by osmosis.

"As a young man, though, I wasn't interested in woodwork," David continues. "Instead I headed for college and a career in the computer industry. In the early days, that was an exciting field: everything was innovative and experimental. After a while, though, it got bogged down in competitiveness. Thanks to my woodworking hobby, when it became obvious to me that I had to leave the computer industry, I had somewhere else to go."

David's woodworking activities have included architectural remodeling, notably the restoration of a home dating from 1760. He remarks that "as woodworking projects go, houses are pretty major, so I decided to focus on smaller objects. I love Art Deco, and I've always had the desire to explore a more sculpted look, rather than the rectangular shapes of more traditional joinery.

Part	Description	Dimensions	Quantity
A	Short leg	1" diameter x $2\frac{7}{8}$"	1
B	Second leg	1" diameter x $5\frac{3}{8}$"	1
C	Third leg	1" diameter x 7"	1
D	Long leg	1" diameter x $7\frac{7}{8}$"	1
E	Container	$1\frac{3}{4}$" x 5" x 7"	3
F	Dowel	$\frac{1}{4}$" x $1\frac{1}{8}$"	5
G	Container lid	$\frac{1}{4}$" x 5" x $5\frac{1}{2}$"	3
H	Lid mirror (not drawn)	4" diameter	1

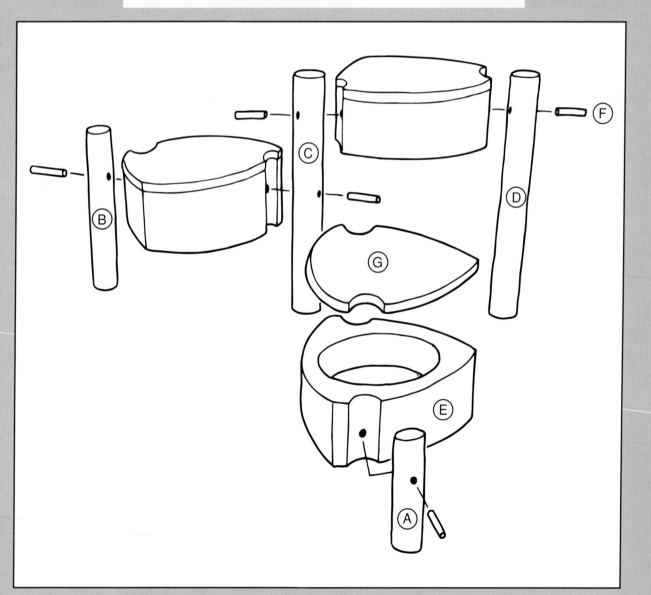

Photo by Boyd Photography

Ken Shepard

Since his retirement twenty years ago, Ken Shepard has been busier than ever pursuing his first love, woodworking. He remembers, "In 1924, when I was eleven, I built myself a darkroom. It was my first project using wood, and I've wanted to return to woodworking ever since. Truth to tell, it took me more than fifty years to get back.

"First I went into the family business, which went bankrupt during the Depression. During the 1930s and 1940s, as our three children came along, I held a variety of jobs: with a mortgage firm, a bus company, and as manager of a diaper service. Eventually I became a civilian employee of the Navy, managing shore facilities, and finally, in 1976, I was able to retire and resume woodworking where I left off."

Ken's skills improved considerably during the break, in part because he repaired and restored antiques off and on over the years. "I still do some restoration, but now mostly I concentrate on making boxes and on lathe work. I'll accept an occasional commission, like a lectern I did recently for a community group."

Ken adds, "When woodworkers ask me for advice, I always tell them two things. First, never compromise on quality. Second, assuming you have some talent to begin with, learn to price things properly. I was so Depression-oriented that I never priced things high enough. Now what I say to people coming up is—recognize the value of your services."

Rosewood Box

Photo on page 63. Exploded diagram on page 62.

This classic design combines the easy access of a hinged lid with the storage capacity of a drawer box in which the lid opens to reveal the top drawer. The box is made from Brazilian rosewood, a species that is no longer available; the logs that provided the raw material have been seasoning in Ken's shop since before the Second World War.

• Join the sides to the back with ³/₈" finger joints. Set sides and back in a rabbet in the ³/₄"-thick mahogany bottom.
• Glue the sides, back, bottom, drawer platform, and top rail together.
• Cut the curved detail in the base parts with a band saw. Miter and assemble base. Glue box to the base.
• Profile the edges of the lid and the drawer fronts with a router. Attach the lid to the box with a continuous hinge.
• Make a ¹/₄" x ³/₄" x 10" rail to place on the back of the box directly beneath the hinge (not shown in diagram). This provides support for the weight of the open lid.
• Attach the sides of the drawers to the drawer body front and back with screws. Use screws to reinforce the connections between drawer body and drawer front.
• Veneer the exposed front edge of the bottom with the same rosewood as the body of the box.
• Mill ¹/₈" dadoes in the drawer sides for the dividers. Section the bottom drawers with three ¹/₈"-thick divider rails. Detail the dividers so that they echo the scrolled profile of the chest base.
• Make two rails for the top drawer running front to back, to be set on either side of a central, velvet-lined ring/bracelet holder (not

drawn, but shown in photo on facing page).

• Varnish the entire box with three coats.

• Attach delicately lathe-turned ebony knobs to the lid and the two drawers.

• Line bottom drawer with velvet. Place ring/bracelet holder in top drawer.

Part	Description	Dimensions	Quantity
A	Side	$\frac{5}{8}$" x $6\frac{1}{4}$" x $7\frac{3}{8}$"	2
B	Back	$\frac{5}{8}$" x $6\frac{1}{4}$" x $11\frac{5}{8}$"	1
C	Bottom	$\frac{3}{4}$" x $7\frac{1}{2}$" x $11\frac{5}{8}$"	1
D	Base front/back	$\frac{3}{4}$" x 1" x $12\frac{1}{8}$"	2
E	Base side	$\frac{3}{4}$" x 1" x $7\frac{7}{8}$"	2
F	Drawer platform	$\frac{1}{4}$" x $6\frac{3}{4}$" x $10\frac{3}{4}$"	1
G	Top rail front	$\frac{1}{4}$" x $\frac{3}{8}$" x $11\frac{5}{8}$"	1
H	Top rail sides	$\frac{1}{4}$" x $\frac{3}{8}$" x $6\frac{1}{2}$"	2
J	Lid	$\frac{3}{4}$" x $7\frac{3}{4}$" x $12\frac{3}{4}$"	1
K	Turned knob	$\frac{5}{8}$" x $\frac{5}{8}$" x $\frac{7}{8}$"	3
L	Hinge	1" x $11\frac{1}{2}$"	1
M	Drawer side	$\frac{5}{16}$" x $2\frac{3}{8}$" x $6\frac{1}{2}$"	4
N	Drawer body front	$\frac{5}{16}$" x $2\frac{3}{8}$" x $9\frac{1}{2}$"	2
O	Drawer front	$\frac{1}{2}$" x $2\frac{3}{8}$" x $10\frac{1}{4}$"	2
P	Drawer body back	$\frac{5}{16}$" x $2\frac{3}{8}$" x $9\frac{7}{8}$"	2
Q	Screw	#6 x $\frac{3}{4}$"	16
R	Drawer divider	$\frac{1}{8}$" x 2" x $5\frac{7}{8}$"	3

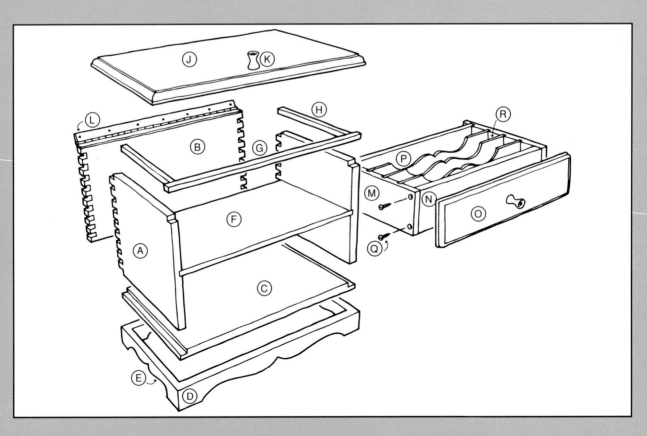

Photo by Elke Freccia

Lorenzo Freccia

"Although wood has been my medium of choice, to highlight a beautiful piece of wood, or merely to showcase technique, has never been of great interest to me," writes Lorenzo Freccia from his New England studio. "Instead, I strive for new and imaginative design approaches.

"My greatest satisfaction comes from creating pieces that offer an element of surprise: a box that opens in an unexpected way, a shape you wouldn't expect to see in wood, or a radically novel design for a familiar object," he continues.

Lorenzo was raised and educated in Italy. He emigrated to the United States to attend M.I.T., and after receiving his Bachelor's and Master's degrees, he worked for many years as a chemist and mathematics teacher. He learned traditional joinery techniques during an intensive course of study in furniture making at the Rhode Island School of Design.

Lorenzo has been a full-time designer/craftsman since 1986, and his work is exhibited at galleries, museums, and shows throughout the country. Lathe turning has become his specialty, and every one of the pieces he makes today is either turned, or contains turned elements.

Turned Half-Moon Box

Exploded diagram on page 66.

Like much of Lorenzo's work, this box is produced on the lathe.

- Cut five 12"-long pieces in sequence from a single 12" wide x 1³/₄" thick board. Plane to appropriate thickness.
- Turn wood to produce the base, top, upper compartment, and two pairs of drawers.
- Make the delicate profile of the lid and the

65

detailing on the vertical
edges on a lathe.

• Cut the resulting circular
forms into two semicircles,
which yield the blanks for
the two boxes.

• Hollow out the drawers
and upper compartment
with a router.

• Drill parts A, B, and C
for the pivot pins.

• Assemble the lid, minus
the base. While assem-
bling, Part E (rear
support) should be
attached to span the
gap produced by the
two layers of drawers.

• Hinge the lid with
tap-in barrel hinges.

• Line the drawers
and upper compart-
ment with black
spray-on flocking.

Part	Description	Dimensions	Quantity
A	Upper compartment	1½" x 5½" x 11"	1
B	Drawer	1½" x 5½" x 5½"	4
C	Base	⅝" x 5½" x 11"	1
D	Lid	1½" x 5½" x 11"	1
E	Rear support	½" x 1½" x 5¼"	1
F	Drawer pivot pin	¼" x 3½"	2
G	Support attachment pins	⅛" x ½"	2
H	Barrel hinge	⅜" diameter	2

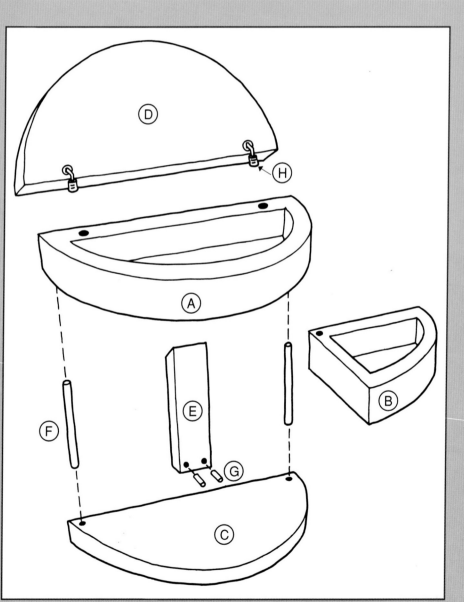

Lorenzo Freccia

Biography on page 65.

Triangle & Circle Box

Photo on page 69. Exploded diagram on page 68.

- Begin with an 8"-square block of 1³/₄"-thick maple. Turn block on a lathe to produce the round shape, hollowed interior, and bead-and-grove detailing on the exterior surface of the box.
- Make an 8" circular lid from ziricote on the lathe.
- Saw the lid and box body into three pieces. Glue each back together with the foot/divider and handle parts in place.
- Cut a 1¹/₄" long x ⁵/₁₆" deep notch into the maple rim of the body.
- Drill the hinge leaves for the hinge pin and attachment screws. Assemble hinge. Screw hinge into the body and the lid.
- Cut the ends of Parts B and D (foot/divider and handle) so that they nest when the box is closed.

Triangle & CIrcle Box

67

Part	Description	Dimensions	Quantity
A	Body	$1^{3}/_{4}$" x 8" x 8"	1
B	Foot/divider	$^{3}/_{8}$" x $2^{1}/_{8}$" x $9^{1}/_{2}$"	2
C	Lid	$^{3}/_{8}$" x 8" x 8"	1
D	Handle	$^{3}/_{8}$" x 1" x $9^{1}/_{2}$"	2
E	Hinge leaf	$^{5}/_{16}$" x $^{3}/_{8}$" x $1^{5}/_{8}$"	1
F	Hinge leaf	$^{5}/_{16}$" x $^{5}/_{8}$" x $^{7}/_{8}$"	2
G	Wood screws	#6 x $^{5}/_{8}$"	4
H	Hinge pin	$^{1}/_{16}$" x $^{3}/_{4}$"	1

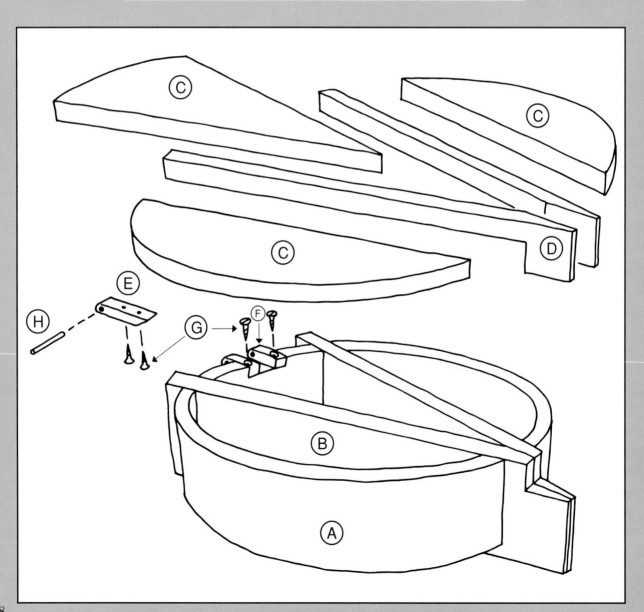

Robert Leung

Robert Leung was born in mainland China. When the Communists came to power, his family moved to Hong Kong. At the age of thirteen, Robert came to the United States, where both his parents had earned university degrees. His interest in wood began in the mid-1970s, when he started making furniture for himself.

Robert writes, "I studied philosophy in college, then worked as a program planner for a chain of movie theaters. My goal was to become a writer, but after a year traveling in Europe, I found myself back in California—and I needed furniture. My first designs were made from soft woods, laboriously cut out using a coping saw. Something about the wood-work I had seen in museums appealed to me, and I began taking courses in art and woodworking at the local branch of the California State University system. The technical skills I gained there made it possi-

Deco Box with Hand Mirror

70

ble for me to begin earning my living as a woodworker.

"Today my work is divided about equally between boxes and commissions for furniture and architectural interiors," he continues. "I can't point to any single source as the inspiration for my designs, but I do like the whimsical. The colors and shapes of the paintings of Paul Klee, as well as their humor, have always appealed to me."

Deco Box with Hand Mirror

Photo and exploded diagram specifications on page 72.

Robert Leung's skill with a lathe has enabled him to blend turned and linear forms in this fascinating design. It combines elements of Futurism and Art Deco with a three-dimensional presence reminiscent of the late work of America's greatest architect, Frank Lloyd Wright.

Despite its eclectic echoes, this maple and walnut box has the classic simplicity that is the hallmark of all good design.

• Mill the individual parts for the top, bottom, back, side blocks, and swing-out drawers.
• Make the drawers' irregularly shaped hollows with a band saw. Sand with a drum sander attachment on a drill press.
• Glue $\frac{1}{8}$"-thick plywood bottoms in place (not shown in drawing). Drill drawers for Part L (brass pin).
• Mill a semi-circular depression in either end of Part H

(back), to allow finger access for the drawers.
• Slightly round the front edges of each side block (Part G) on the side closest to the swing-out drawer.
• Finish-sand the interiors of all parts.
• Assemble box with glue. When dry, perfect the oval shape of the box using a 6" x 48" belt sander with progressively finer grits.
• Attach the sides of the center drawer to the back with a

single dovetail. Attach to the front with dowels that reinforce the rabbet joint.
• Attach the turned drawer handle with reinforcing dowels.
• Turn Parts E, A, and C (circular top compartment and the two components that make up the lid) on a lathe.
• Attach the handle to the mirror back with an invisible $\frac{1}{4}$" dowel.
• Line drawers with taupe ultrasuede.

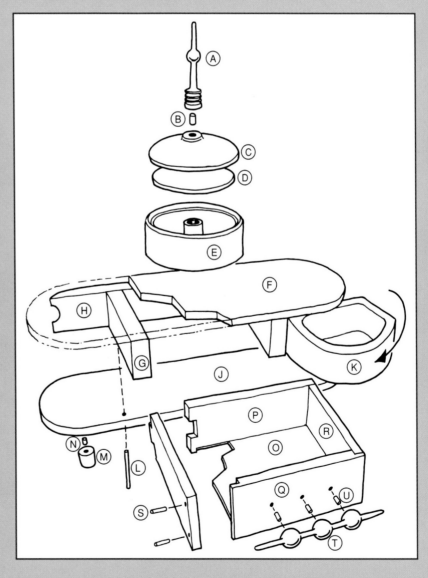

71

Part	Description	Dimensions	Quantity
A	Handle	$3/4" \times 3/4" \times 3^1/2"$	1
B	Dowel	$1/4" \times 1/4"$	1
C	Mirror back	$3/4" \times 4" \times 4"$	1
D	Mirror	3" diameter	1
E	Top compartment	$1^3/4" \times 4^5/8" \times 4^5/8"$	1
F	Top	$3/8" \times 5^3/4" \times 14^7/8"$	1
G	Side block	$1" \times 1^3/4" \times 5^3/8"$	2
H	Back	$3/8" \times 1^3/4" \times 11^3/4"$	1
J	Bottom	$1/4" \times 5^3/4" \times 14^7/8"$	1
K	Swing-out drawer	$1^3/4" \times 4" \times 5^3/8"$	2
L	Brass pin	$1/8" \times 2^1/8"$	2
M	Foot	$5/8" \times 3/4"$	4
N	Dowel	$1/8" \times 1/4"$	4
O	Center drawer bottom	$1/8" \times 4^5/8" \times 5"$	1
P	Center drawer back	$3/8" \times 1^3/4" \times 5"$	1
Q	Center drawer front	$1/2" \times 1^3/4" \times 5"$	1
R	Center drawer side	$1/2" \times 1^3/4" \times 5^3/8"$	2
S	Dowel	$1/8" \times 5/8"$	4
T	Center drawer handle	$5/8" \times 5/8" \times 4^7/8"$	1
U	Dowel	$1/8" \times 1/4"$	3

Al Ladd

Al Ladd first became interested in woodworking after he landed a job in a production furniture shop. "I had always thought I'd be a teacher. Unfortunately, my state de-funded education while I was in college. Since I had worked as a carpenter's helper, I knew something about wood, and the furniture job showed me what incredible results you could get if you had the right machinery."

What fascinates Al most about woodworking is the way gluing together different species, with their varying grain and color combinations, can produce an infinite variety of patterns. He writes from his Massachusetts studio, "I have a nephew who loves turtles, and while I was at the furniture shop, I made him a turtle-shaped checkerboard. That was my first introduction to edge gluing end-grain squares. It came out so well that I began making cutting boards.

End-Grain Lid Box

"End-grain makes a lot of sense for a functional project like a cutting board," Al explains, "because it's so much harder than the face grain. But the patterns I was creating were so beautiful that I wanted to use them more, and that led me to apply my end-grain approach to jewelry boxes. Through trial and error, I've developed a whole series of techniques for making designs like the one in the box shown; as I go on, the boxes keep getting more intricate and more amazing all the time."

End-Grain Lid Box

Photos on pages 73 and 76.

The main event in this design is the lid panel, an intricate assembly of square and half-square blocks, each of which contains a nested set of crescent moon shapes in three contrasting woods: boxwood, oak, and walnut.

• This box is a traditional mitered design. Glue up the body and lid as a single rectangular solid, 5" high. Slice the lid off on a table saw (see page 12).

• Reinforce the miter joint by using a butterfly-shaped spline, glued into a slot on the face of each miter. Mill both the spline and its slot using a router with a small dovetail bit. The spline is visible on the bottom of the box, but not on the top; it stops $1/4$" before the upper edge of each side.

• The tray rests on two rails. Mill each with a keel that is glued into a $1/8$" saw kerf slot

milled on the insides of the front and back.

• Use brass barrel hinges to operate the lid. The lid is held open by a sliding brass lid support.

• The crescent moon shapes in the lid are produced from 10"-long, $3/8$"- and $1/4$"-diameter half-dowels. Turn dowels on a lathe and then rip. Glue into $3/8$"- and $1/4$"-diameter semicircular profiles router cut into opposing faces of $3/4$"-square 10"-long rails.

• Once the complex millwork

is finished, assemble the resulting $3/4$"-square rails with other elements, including a walnut border and a $1/32$" stripe detail made from guitar rosette material.

• Crosscut this final 10"-long assembly into sections $1/4$" thick. Sand. Each section is an identical panel containing the complex design.

Part	Description	Dimensions	Quantity
A	Front/back	$5/8$" x $3^1/4$" x 10"	2
B	Side	$5/8$" x $3^1/4$" x $8^1/4$"	2
C	Bottom	$1/4$" x $7^3/4$" x $9^1/2$"	1
D	Spline	$1/4$" x $3/8$" x $4^3/4$"	4
E	Tray rail	$1/4$" x $1/2$" x 8"	2
F	Lid side	$5/8$" x $1^5/8$" x $8^1/4$"	2
G	Lid front/back	$5/8$" x $1^5/8$" x 10"	2
H	Lid top panel	$1/4$" x $7^1/2$" x 9"	1
J	Handle	$3/8$" x $1/2$" x $2^1/4$"	1
K	Handle pins	$1/8$" x $1/4$"	2
L	Tray front/back	$3/8$" x $1^1/4$" x $8^3/8$"	2
M	Tray side	$3/8$" x $1^1/4$" x $6^7/8$"	2
N	Tray bottom	$1/8$" x $6^1/2$" x 8"	1
O	Tray dividers	$1/8$" x $7/8$" as req'd	4
P	Barrel hinge	$3/8$" diameter	2
Q	Sliding lid support	as req'd	1

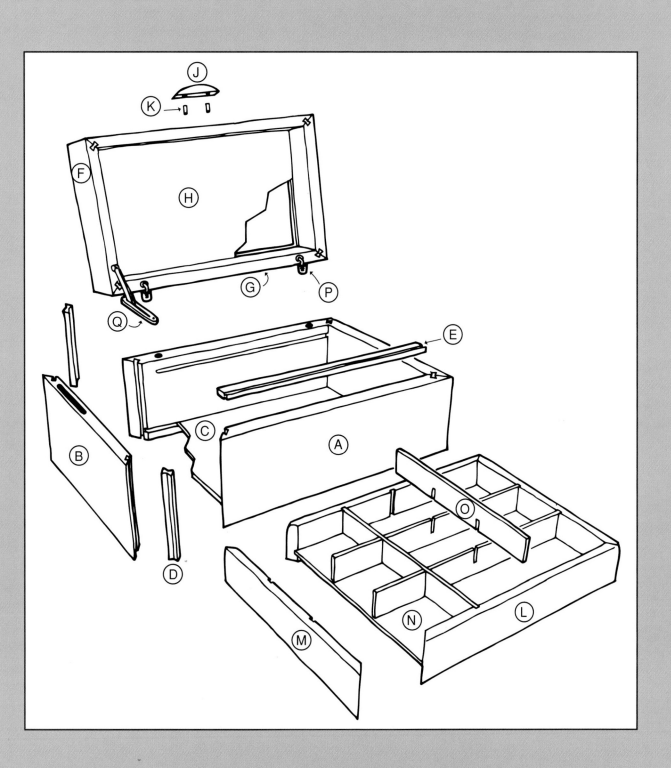

Terry Evans

Photo by Ramaglia/Lutke-Stahlman

Growing up on a Kansas farm, Terry Evans has an early memory of a hand-carved stone watering trough, created by a family member in the early part of the century. "The care and concern that went into making that trough became part of my heritage," Terry explains. "As I got older, I noticed the same qualities in other objects. I was especially impressed by the fine harness work I saw, and that got me interested in making things out of leather."

By the time he was in college, Terry had developed into an enthusiastic leather-smith. He writes, "My leather work provided me with pocket change all during college. Not long afterward, it paid the hospital bill when Mauna and I had our first child."

It was not until Terry began making inlaid wooden belt buckles for his leather belts that his interest shifted to wood. "I'd always loved beautiful and

Inlaid Lid Box

exotic wood, and I would meet collectors with literally thousands of species. Most of the time I could only get hold of small pieces, and that's why I've tended to work on a small scale ever since. The free, asymmetrical geometry of the great nonobjective painter Wassily Kandinsky was my greatest inspiration."

While evolving his unique style of inlay, Terry has continued to serve as a full-time art teacher in the Kansas public schools. Although he has taught many subjects in the art curriculum, he currently teaches photography, and the photo of him was taken by two of his students.

Inlaid lid box

Photos on pages 77 and 80.

Terry has perfected his own style of intricate three-dimensional inlay that is based on traditional marquetry, but creates an effect that is both more dramatic and more expressive of the artist's individual aesthetic vision. The elegant design and careful joinery of his lacewood jewelry box are a perfect complement to the lid inlay.

The lid inlay itself is a mosaic of geometric forms, including both natural colors and brightly dyed woods. Set in careful counterpoint, six irregular pillow-like shapes rise from neatly carved depressions, like strange hills on a plain of dreams. Terry's long study of wooden jewelry making gave him the skills to create these intricate designs on such an intimate scale. Some of the raw materials he uses come from suppliers of guitar rosettes and purfling; others he fabricates himself.

• The body of the box is a conventional mitered design. Prior to glue-up, mill a rabbet in the upper edge of each side to hold the lid, and cut saw kerf slots for Part D, the nearly invisible reinforcing splines.

• Although the bottom can be made of $1/8"$ or $1/4"$ plywood, Terry prefers to use a solid piece of $1/4"$ thick lacewood.

Part	Description	Dimensions	Quantity
A	Front/back	$7/8" \times 2^1/4" \times 14^7/8"$	2
B	Side	$7/8" \times 2^1/4" \times 7^3/4"$	2
C	Bottom	$1/4" \times 6^1/2" \times 13^1/2"$	1
D	Spline	$1/8" \times 1/4" \times 1^3/4"$	4
E	Foot	$1" \times 1" \times 1"$	4
F	Lid rail front/back	$1/2" \times 1^1/4" \times 13^5/8"$	2
FF	Lacewood lid panel	$1/4" \times 4^1/4" \times 11^5/8"$	1
G	Lid rail side	$1/2" \times 1^1/4" \times 6^1/4"$	2
H	Hinge pin	$1/16" \times 3/4"$	2
J	Border rail front/back	$1/8" \times 1/8" \times 11^1/8"$	2
K	Border rail sides	$1/8" \times 1/8" \times 3^3/4"$	2
L	Inlay support	$1/8" \times 3^3/4" \times 11^1/8"$	1
M	Lid inlay: raised elements	n/a	as req'd
N	Divider front/back	$1/8" \times 1^1/2" \times 13^1/8"$	2
O	Divider side	$1/8" \times 1^1/2" \times 6"$	2
P	Divider separators	$1/8" \times 1^1/2"$	as req'd
Q	Lid lift	$5/16" \times 3/4" \times 2^1/2"$	1
R	Lift pins	$1/8" \times 1/4"$	3

Feather the edges so that they fit into the ⅛" saw kerf dado.

 Profile Part FF (lacewood lid panel) in the same manner, feathering down in thickness to fit into the ⅛" dado. This detail, subtly noticeable when the box is opened, is visible in the photo on page 80.

 For added strength, use mortise and tenon joinery to connect the short sides of the lid to the long sides..

 Finish-sand the inside of the box and both sides of the lid.

 Drill holes in the end of the lid and the inside of the sides for the hinge pins. The holes should not penetrate through to the outside of the box; so the lid must be installed at the time the box is glued up. Do not drill the pin holes deeper than ¼" into the sides, as much of their thickness will be cut away in the next step.

 Glue up the box. After the glue is dry, angle the table saw blade and mill the bevels on the box sides. Finish-sand

on a belt sander.

 Make each of the four feet from two sections of profiled rail. Miter and glue together to form a 90 degree angle.

 Carve the gap in the front.

 Shape the lid lift on a belt sander. Install.

 Place lid design in lid.

 Oil, wax, and buff box.

 Carefully glue a piece of leather in the bottom. Place the dividers on top of it, neatly covering the edges of the leather.

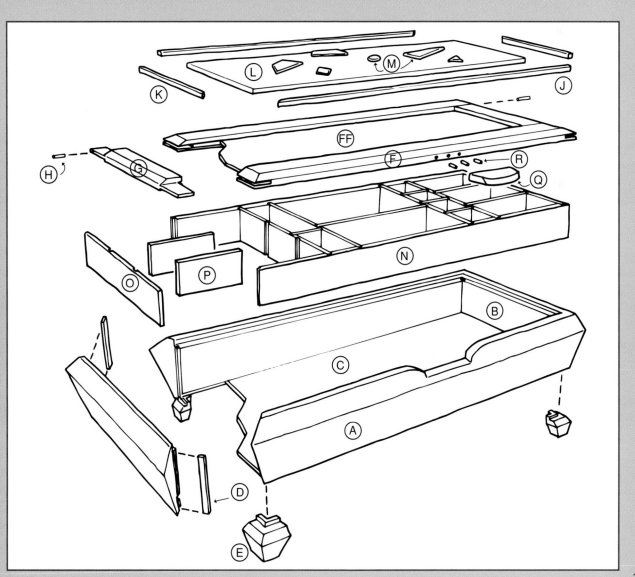

Photo by Yukako Carr

Robert Brackbill

Robert earned his captain's license and went on to skipper the Fairwind as a snorkel-and-dive business off the Kona Coast of the "Big Island," where he lives today.

It wasn't long before he discovered koa wood and became fascinated with box-making. "I call my work ho'ala, which means "to awaken" in Hawaiian," Robert explains. "Compared to working on boats or houses, boxes are more manageable, and I enjoy the challenge of getting it just right. I never liked boxes with drawers that fall out when they're opened, so I developed my slide mechanism that allows full extension. It took me three months of experimentation, but it's a solution that really works."

Koa Chest

Photo on page 81. Exploded diagram on page 84.

This gemlike chest derives its beauty from two elements: Robert Brackbill's use of dramatic curly Hawaiian koa, and the meticulous detailing of his design.

Born in the coastal town of Santa Cruz, California, Robert Brackbill was first introduced to woodworking in high school. After a series of summer jobs as an apprentice carpenter, a friend asked Robert to help him build a sailboat to sail around the world. During the five years it took to complete the boat, Robert acquired two sets of useful skills: finish woodworking and marine carpentry, and—thanks to service in the Merchant Marine—seamanship and navigation.

The young men christened their project the Fairwind, and set sail for Hawaii, first stop on their world tour. One thing led to another, and their cruise never got any farther. However,

Although the bottoms of the compartment and the box are not visible without close inspection, Robert insists on making them from solid $^1/_8$"-thick koa, rather than plywood.

Robert has been careful to preserve the grain pattern that is dramatically visible across the entire front of the box. Keep in mind, however, that highly figured wood such as koa is especially prone to tear-out, even with a sharp carbide bit, so it is essential to back all cuts with solid material.

It is a further testament to the maker's skill that even after sanding, the cut for the drawer front only used $^1/_{16}$" of material.

• Start from a six-sided rectangular solid, with sides $5^5/_8$" high and a delicate $^5/_{16}$" thick.
• Carefully mill finger joints in the ends of the front, back, and two sides using a router jig.
• Band-saw out the drawer front (Part P) after the parts are milled.
• Glue up the body of the box with both bottoms in place.
• Slice off the top on a table saw. The height of one of the finger joints will be reduced by $^1/_8$", the width of a saw kerf.
• Make the trays and divider rails, the lid and drawer handles, the hinges, and the drawer glide pins from Hawaiian milo wood.
• In order for the drawers to extend far enough to make their full depth

accessible, construct koa extension glides. Attach Part L (fixed drawer glide) to the inside of the box. Use a dovetail bit on a router table to create its projecting rail. The channel in Part M fits onto this projecting rail. Part M, in turn, has a projecting rail on which the drawer slides. Part N (glide pin) keeps the moving glide from exiting the box when the drawer is opened. At the same time, Part O (glide

stop) keeps the drawer from exiting.

• Rather than store-bought hardware, this design features handmade wood hinges. Mill stock for the hinges $^3/_8$" thick by $1^3/_4$" wide. Drill a $^1/_8$"-hole for the brass hinge pin. On the router table, mill a finger joint pattern, identical to that used on the sides. Round the projecting fingers, then crosscut to appropriate length for each of the two leaves. Finish-

Part	Description	Dimensions	Quantity
A	Top	$^1/_4$" x $5^3/_8$" x $11^3/_4$"	1
B	Lid front/back	$^5/_{16}$" x 1" x $11^3/_4$"	2
C	Lid side	$^5/_{16}$" x 1" x $5^3/_8$"	2
D	Handle	$^3/_8$" x $^3/_8$" x 8"	2
E	Box side	$^5/_{16}$" x $4^1/_2$" x $5^3/_8$"	2
F	Box front, upper	$^5/_{16}$" x $1^7/_8$" x $11^3/_4$"	1
G	Box front, lower	$^5/_{16}$" x $^3/_4$" x $11^3/_4$"	1
H	Box back	$^5/_{16}$" x $4^1/_2$" x $11^3/_4$"	1
J	Compartment bottom	$^1/_8$" x 5" x $11^1/_4$"	1
K	Box bottom	$^1/_8$" x 5" x $11^1/_4$"	1
L	Fixed drawer glide	$^3/_8$" x $1^3/_4$" x $4^3/_4$"	2
M	Moving drawer glide	$^3/_8$" x $1^3/_4$" x $4^3/_4$"	2
N	Glide pin	$^3/_8$" x $^3/_8$" x $^3/_4$" plus dowel	2
O	Glide stop	$^1/_8$" x $^1/_2$"	2
P	Drawer front	$^5/_{16}$" x $1^3/_4$" x $11^3/_4$"	1
Q	Drawer side	$^3/_8$" x $1^3/_4$" x $4^3/_4$"	2
R	Drawer back	$^5/_{16}$" x $1^3/_4$" x $9^7/_8$"	1
S	Drawer bottom	$^1/_8$" x $4^5/_8$" x $9^7/_8$"	1
T	Lower hinge leaf	$^3/_8$" x $1^3/_4$" x $2^1/_4$"	2
U	Upper hinge leaf	$^3/_8$" x $1^3/_4$" x $1^1/_8$"	2
V	Brass hinge pin	$^1/_8$" x $1^3/_4$"	2
W	Tray	$^1/_4$" x 3" x $4^5/_8$"	2
X	Divider rail	$^1/_4$" x $^7/_8$" x $11^1/_8$"	2
Y	Divider rail	$^1/_4$" x $^7/_8$" x $3^5/_{16}$"	2

sand the entire assembly. Insert the pin before the hinge is glued to the box.

• Sand carefully and intensively; highly figured wood like this repays such labor. Follow with a hand-rubbed oil finish, wax, and buffing. Line the drawer, trays, and compartment with velvet (see page 11).

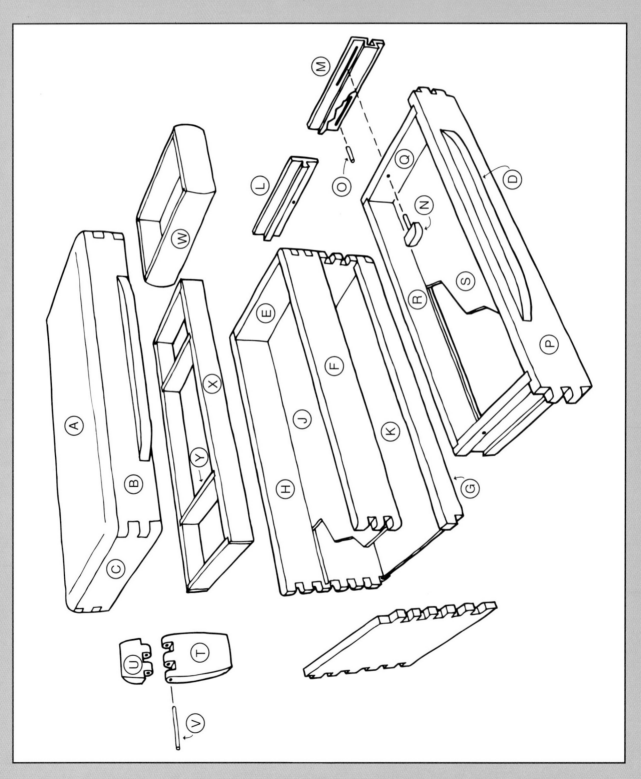

T. Breeze VerDant

Photo by Allan W. Gill

"I have a long history with trees," Breeze recalls. *"As a child, I could always be found up in them. As an adult, I logged them to build myself a log cabin, and to produce enough firewood to see me through the long Adirondack winters. I never cease to be awed by trees, by their inward and outward beauty, and respectful of the essential role they play in all aspects of our life.*

"I've been a student in many different settings," says Breeze, *"including the school of hard knocks, from which these boxes should earn me a doctoral degree."* His formal education as a woodworker came during study with master marquetry artist Silas Kopf. Breeze continues, *"Marquetry allows me to be creative with wood; I get to work with the natural enchantment of so many different species. I like the fact that while my work celebrates trees, it has a min-*

Magnolia Marquetry Box

85

imal impact on them. I use native hardwoods, like poplar, sycamore, cherry, holly, and maple, and scrap and cutoffs whenever I can.

"Marquetry is an ancient craft, one that combines the natural and the artistic in a way that I like. With it, I feel I've found a chance to achieve my goal: to stun people with the beauty of wood grain, and be happy doing it."

Magnolia Marquetry Box

Photo on page 85.

The dramatic impact of this box comes from its elongated shape, the unusual beveled and slipfeathered detailing of the four corners, and most of all, from the marvellous lifelike quality of the floral marquetry design of the top.

This design represents a magnolia blossom, made from maple and sycamore, set in a field of poplar burl. Its leaves are tulipwood, purpleheart, koa, narra, ebony, Goncalo Alves, and satinwood, each meticulously cut and inserted in a seamless design. The organic energy of the floral motif is set against a geometric grid of three ebony lines, punctuated by $1/4$" tulipwood circles. In this otherwise tightly symmetrical design, the artist has carefully placed the magnolia blossom slightly off-center.

- The mitered box body is made of walnut. Glue the box and lid up as a single piece, with $2^7/8$"-high sides.
- Mill slipfeather slots in each corner. Follow the technique on page 10, with two modifications. First, slightly tilt the table saw blade so that the slots are cut at an angle. Second, make the slipfeathers from two pieces of contrasting $1/8$"-thick wood, $1/4$" and 1" wide, respectively (the slipfeathers will be two-tone). Glue the pieces together on edge.
- Use a 6" x 48" belt sander or 10" disc sander to remove excess slipfeather material and glue, and to create the corner bevel.

• Rip the lid of the box off with a table saw.

• Install a ⅛"-thick liner (Parts C and D) that extends slightly above the rim of the box body. This will hold the lid in place and provide a snug fit. Round the top edge of the liner slightly.

• Set the lid inlay on a base of Baltic birch plywood. Detail the edge with a ¼" x ¼" band of rosewood.

Part	Description	Dimensions	Quantity
A	Front/back	½" x 2" x 12"	2
B	Side	½" x 2" x 3¾"	2
C	Liner front/back	⅛" x 1⅞" x 11"	2
D	Liner side	⅛" x 1⅞" x 2¾"	2
E	Lid front/back	½" x ¾" x 12"	2
F	Lid side	½" x ¾" x 3¾"	2
G	Top	¼" x 3¾" x 12"	1
H	Slipfeather	⅛" x 1¼" x 1¼"	8
J	Bottom	⅛" x 3" x 11⅜"	1

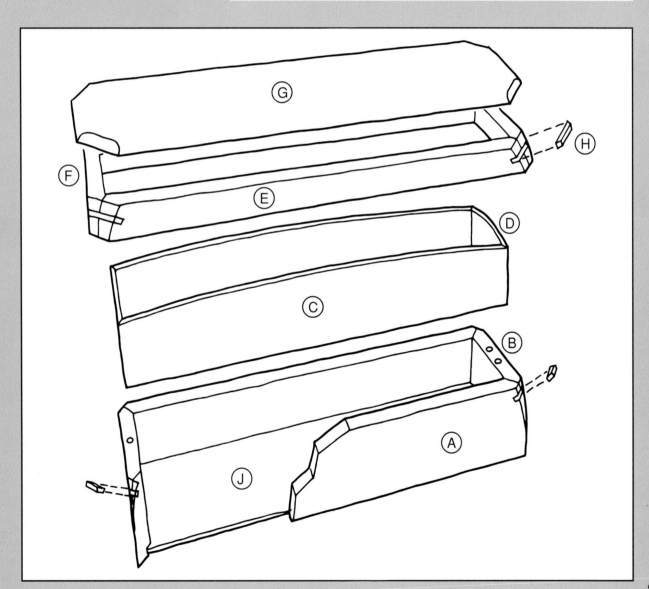

Twin Lid Box

indigenous to the region," he says. "The variety of colors, forms, and combinations you find in wood is just fascinating, and I hope someday to be able to spend all my time working with it."

Twin Lid Box

Photo and exploded diagram on page 90.

The gem-like quality of this small jewelry box comes from an unusually shaped block of Idaho walnut, harvested and kiln-dried by the box-maker.

This box is built using band-saw box techniques, in which parts are sawn and later glued back together in such a way as to produce all but invisible seams.

• Start with a $3^{1}/_{4}$"-thick block, $3^{1}/_{2}$" wide by 7" long. Rip the block into two pieces, each about $1^{1}/_{2}$" thick.
• Cut off both sets of end blocks (Parts B and C). Cut off the two lids.
• Band-saw out the interior of the box body.
• Drill holes in the edges of the lids and the inside face of the end blocks for the hinge pins.
• Round the inside back edge of each body to allow its lid to swing.
• Polish the interior surfaces.
• Assemble lids, body, and end blocks at the same time.

Roger Lee

Roger Lee is the third generation in his family to love woodworking. As a boy he spent as much time as he could around his grandfather's workshop, and his father, John Lee, is a woodworker whose "Pandora's Boxes" are featured on page 94.

"In addition to what I'd observed at home," Roger recalls, "two semesters of junior high woodshop kindled the fire. I got sidetracked by sports and studies during high school, but after graduating I began producing Christmas presents for the family. Soon people outside the family were offering to pay for my work, and a business was born."

With a degree in economics and a job as economic development director for an Oregon community, woodworking time for Roger is limited. "I've traveled a lot, and whenever I'm exploring a new part of the globe, the first thing I do is find out what kind of timber is

Part	Description	Dimensions	Quantity
A	Box body	$1^{1}/_{2}$" x $3^{1}/_{2}$" x $5^{1}/_{2}$"	2
B	Outer end block	$1^{1}/_{8}$" x $1^{1}/_{2}$" x $3^{1}/_{2}$"	2
C	Inner end block	$5/_{8}$" x $1^{1}/_{2}$" x $1^{1}/_{2}$"	2
D	Lid	$1/_{4}$" x $3^{1}/_{4}$" x $5^{1}/_{2}$"	2
E	Hinge pin	$1/_{16}$" x $1/_{4}$"	4

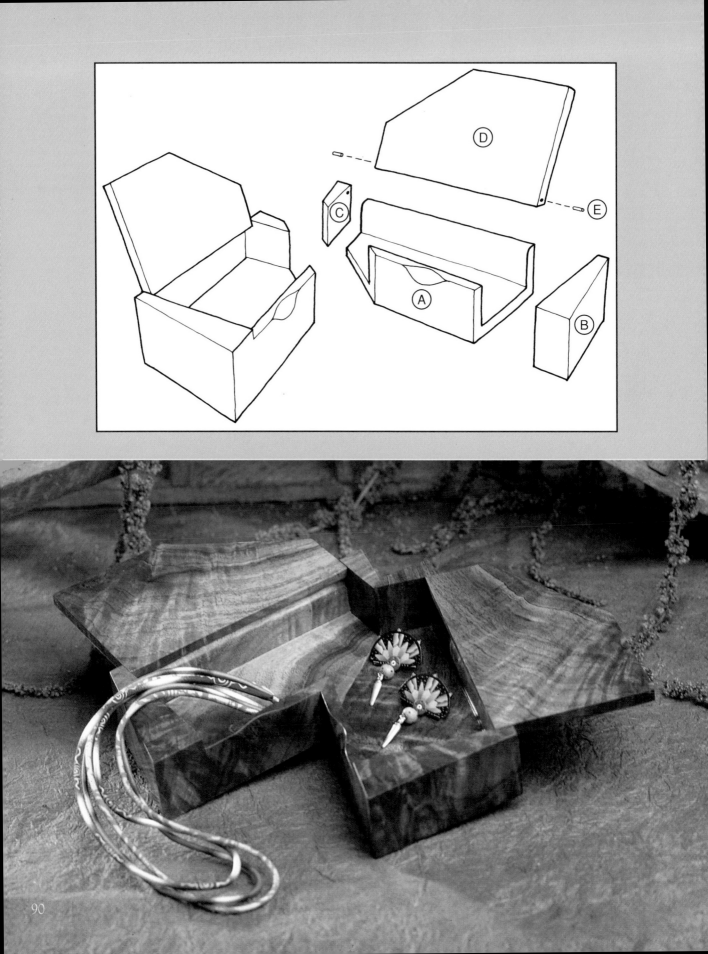

Roger Lee

Biography on page 89.

Seashell Box

Photo on page 91.

This unusual box was made from two pieces cut from a 2"-thick plank of rosewood. At the edges of this plank, the naturally light colored sapwood was once inhabited by borer beetles, and Roger has deliberately included these irregularities.

Roger observes, "This one-of-a-kind container is rather low-tech, but it sure was time-intensive!"

• With the two shell halves still in square form, cut the $^3/_8$" hinge slots with a dado blade. Drill for the hinge pin.
• Hollow out the interior of the box, using rasps, power grinding burrs, and an orbital sander.
• Carve the exterior with chisels and gouges.
• Glue the square ends of the hinge blocks into the upper shell. Attach the upper shell to the lower shell with the hinge pin.
• Plug the ends of the pin hole.
• Finish the box with multiple thin coats of carnauba wax.

Part	Description	Dimensions	Quantity
A	Lower shell	2" x 6$^1/_2$" x 7$^1/_2$"	1
B	Upper shell	2" x 6$^1/_2$" x 7$^1/_2$"	1
C	Hinge block	$^3/_8$" x $^5/_8$" x 1$^3/_4$"	4
D	Hinge pin	$^1/_{16}$" x 3$^1/_2$"	1
E	Plug	$^1/_{16}$" x $^1/_{16}$"	2

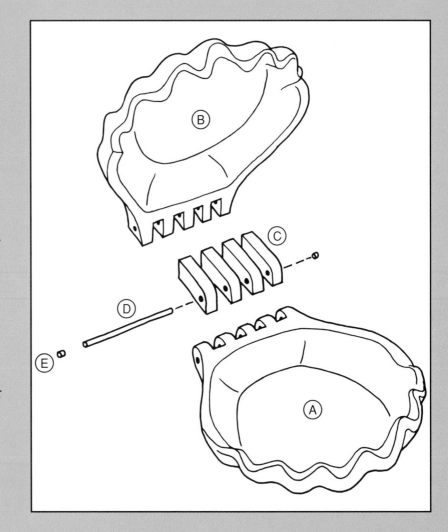

John C. Lee

"We always had a small woodshop as I was growing up on our dairy farm in southern Idaho. When I went to Colorado State University to become a veterinarian, I took odd jobs and worked as a photographer, but even so, from time to time, I had to sell off part of our dairy herd to pay expenses. Over the next thirty years, as my wife and I managed a veterinary practice and raised four children, my time for both photography and woodworking was severely limited," John Lee writes.

"When my dad died, I bought some of his old woodworking equipment and began building a few projects. But it wasn't until a serious illness prevented my son Roger from returning to high school for his senior year that we really got going on boxes. I could see I'd have to retire from my practice to devote full time to our wood projects and my photography. That was nine years ago, and the creative rush has never slowed down!

"My Pandora's Boxes," John continues, "are inspired by a design the Singer Sewing Company produced around 1889 to hold some of their attachments.

"I enjoy the whole process of woodworking—the smell, the beauty, and the feel of wood, the challenge of designing—as much as the final product. Even though I have plenty of regular lumber, I'm constantly retrieving logs from the firewood pile: with every good-looking piece of wood I find, I can see a box inside, begging me to let it out."

Pandora's Boxes

Photo on page 97. Exploded diagram on page 96.

The ingenious design of this set of three nested boxes is based on hinging together the top, bottom, front, and back. When the box is completely opened, it is no longer a box at all, but rather four flat surfaces, connected by three sets of hinges, each with an equilateral triangle at either end. The woods used are birdseye maple, padouk, madrone, wenge, and highly figured walnut; dimensions shown are for the largest of the three.

Because of its intricacy, it is advisable to experiment with this design using scrap ¼" plywood. Once the concept is clear, a finished version can be produced in fine hardwood.

- Connect the triangular sides to Parts A and B with ¼" finger joints.
- The hinges consist of two identical blocks (Parts D and E) connected by a ¹⁄₁₆"-diameter pin (Part F).
- Cut the hinge slots with a router using a dovetail bit. Give the blocks a matching dovetail shape.
- Assemble each hinge before gluing in. As shown in the drawing on page 96, the end of Part E is flush with the rounded edge of the top. Part D extends ¼" beyond the edge so that it can fit into its corresponding slot.
- Carve the triangular slot into the front. Carve the latch.
- The latch pivots on a pin held by two blocks. The latch assembly is installed complete. When closed, the latch will lie in the triangular slot.

Part	Description	Dimensions	Quantity
A	Front/back	$1/4$" x $2^3/4$" x $6^1/4$"	2
B	Top/bottom	$1/4$" x $3^1/8$" x $6^1/4$"	2
C	Side	$1/4$" x $1^1/2$" x $2^3/4$"	8
D	Hinge block	$1/4$" x $3/8$" x $1/2$"	6
E	Hinge block	$1/4$" x $3/8$" x $1/2$"	6
F	Hinge pin	$1/16$" x $3/16$"	6
G	Latch	$1/4$" x $1/2$" x $7/8$"	1
H	Latch block	$1/4$" x $1/4$" x $1/4$"	2
J	Latch pin	$1/16$" x $1/2$"	1

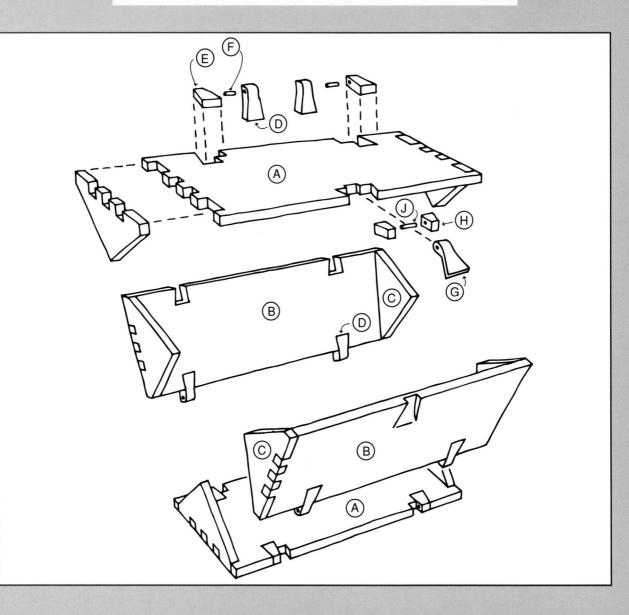

Photo by Dave Kamm

Peter Czuk

Peter Czuk's interest in wood dates to the early 1970s when he and his brothers discovered redwood burls in Northern California. Months were spent salvaging burls from creek beds and beaches. Peter recalls, "We'd rent a truck and drive back to Michigan with seven or eight tons of burls. Fortunately, we found an abandoned company store on an old mint plantation that was large enough to set up shop. The natural shapes of the furniture I produced then had a definite impact on my sense of design."

Today, Peter is known for his contemporary sculptural furniture, boxes, and desk accessories. He reflects, "Over the years, I've combined my love of wood and my fascination with things mechanical. I use a variety of media: wood, glass, alumilite, and brass. My creative challenge is to find new expression in traditional materials.

"The basic table, for example, is simply four legs and a top. I think about how many shapes can be used to replace the four-leg concept, yet still be functional. Success to me is to design a new twist on a familiar design."

Pivot Lid Box

Photo on page 101. Exploded diagram on page 100.

This sculptural box, intended to hold a special gift, is a fascinating assembly of unusual angles and novel materials, with a unique mechanism for hinging the lid. The secret of the opening mechanism lies in the geometry of the triangle formed by the handle, the lid, and the pivot pin. When everything is in proper alignment, the lid will just clear the upper edge of the box as it opens. Use scrap wood to experiment with differing possibilities until you have found the right combination.

You may wish to start with scrap pieces of $^1/_4$" plywood, rough shaping them on the band saw or belt/disc sander to approximate dimensions of the box shown in the drawing and the photographs.

The irregular shapes and angles of Peter's box reflect a careful playfulness, and the same spirit must be present in approaching such a design. Even Peter himself could not exactly duplicate this one-of-a-kind creation, so variations in size, shape, and material are entirely in order.

• Fit the bloodwood body of the box around a white plastic interior and base. Make Part G (bottom liner) from maple burl dyed aquamarine. Make the lid from a solid piece of maple burl.
• Temporarily fasten the lid in place to the glued-up box body. Give the box its exterior shape on a 6" x 48" belt sander. With the lid still in place, drill the hole for the pivot pin.
• Carve the handle from bloodwood.
• Connect the lid to its pivot pin with the handle. Use a $^1/_{16}$"-thick brass plate to reinforce the handle where it is penetrated by the pivot. Attach the handle to the lid with four brass pins, three of which project $^1/_2$" beyond the handle surface.

Part	Description	Dimensions	Quantity
A	Side	$1/4$" x $2^1/8$" x 5"	1
B	Front	$1/4$" x $1^7/8$" x $8^3/4$"	1
C	Side	$7/8$" x $2^1/4$" x 3"	1
D	Back	$1/4$" x $2^3/8$" x $10^1/2$"	1
E	Base	$1/4$" x 5" x $9^1/4$"	1
F	Interior liner	$1^3/8$" x $3^1/2$" x $6^1/4$"	1
G	Bottom liner	$1/4$" x 3" x $5^3/4$"	1
H	Lid	$3/8$" x $6^1/2$" x $3^7/8$"	1
J	Handle	$1/2$" x $1^1/2$" x $5^1/2$"	1
K	Brass pivot pin	$1/8$" x $3^1/2$"	1

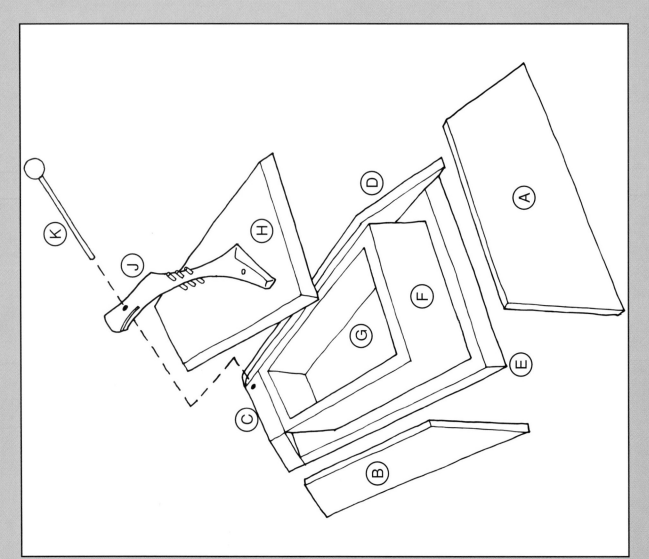

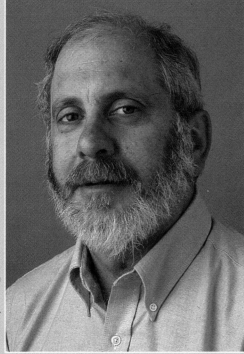

was the most difficult. Since I liked the industrial aspect of production woodwork, solving those problems in wood was a pleasure for me, and that led to my jewelry boxes and silver chests.

"What I like best about what I do is making good things that add value to the world. I build into my boxes details that aren't immediately obvious, and I get letters from customers thanking me for some proportion, some feature they just noticed—three years after they bought the box.

"There are lots of beautiful things in the world, and the best have about them a kind of mystery. Exploring them takes work; it isn't easy, but it's a thrill, for its own sake. That's what drives me; for me, it's the aesthetic principle that unites woodwork, furniture making, and theoretical physics. The real things in the world are the strangest of all."

Mark Rehmar

"I majored in mathematics in college," writes Mark Rehmar from Oregon, "and then studied theoretical physics in graduate school. It wasn't until I had the opportunity to design and build a house in my late twenties that I first discovered how exciting the design process can be. The only formal training I had as a woodworker was a few months' apprenticeship with a furniture maker. Fortunately, by that time, I'd realized the importance of learning how to learn.

"I was fascinated to discover that my current and former areas of interest had something in common. Physics and design seemed to me to be the two disciplines in which solving problems

Part	Description	Dimensions	Quantity
A	Front/back	$5/8$" x $4^1/4$" x $18^3/4$"	2
B	Side	$5/8$" x $4^1/4$" x 15"	2
C	Bottom	$1/4$" x $14^1/4$" x 18"	1
D	Tray rail	$3/4$" x 2" x $17^1/2$"	2
E	Slipfeathers	$1/8$" x $7/8$" x $1^1/2$"	12
F	Lid front rail	$5/8$" x $2^1/2$" x $18^1/8$"	1
FF	Lid rear rail	$5/8$" x $1^1/2$" x $18^1/8$"	1
G	Lid side rail	$5/8$" x $1^1/2$" x 12"	2
H	Top panel	$3/8$" x $11^1/2$" x $15^1/2$"	1
J	Upper tray side	$9/16$" x $7/8$" x $13^5/8$"	2
K	Upper tray side	$9/16$" x $7/8$" x 9"	2
L	Upper tray bottom	$1/8$" x $8^5/8$" x $13^3/8$"	1
M	Lower tray side	$9/16$" x $7/8$" x $12^3/4$"	2
N	Lower tray side	$9/16$" x $7/8$" x 9"	2
O	Lower tray bottom	$1/8$" x $8^5/8$" x $12^1/2$"	1
P	Tray divider rail	$1/8$" x $3/4$" as req'd	4
Q	Tray divider rail	$1/8$" x $5/8$" as req'd	8
R	Hinge pin	$1/8$" x 1"	2

Walnut Chest

Photo on page 102. Exploded diagram specifications on page 103.

The rich beauty of walnut is perfectly shown off in this large-capacity chest. Mark has selected an extraordinary single piece of highly figured walnut for the lid panel.

• This box uses miter joints, reinforced with horizontal slipfeathers of contrasting wood for both box body and trays. See the General Instructions (pages 7–16) for a full explanation of construction details, such as miter joints, slipfeathers, and the invisible pin hinge.

• Mill a $5/16$"-wide and $5/8$"-deep rabbet in the top edge of each of the four sides prior to assembly. The lid will rest on this rabbet.

• Mill two $5/8$" x $2 5/8$" notches in the front for the lid handles.

• Dado the $1/4$" bottom into the sides for added strength.

• Set the lid panel into a dado on all sides. To allow for expansion, do not glue the lid panel. Hold it in place with two $1/16$" brass pins inserted through the rear rail of the frame. The pins should be visible only from the inside. Reduce the panel thickness to $1/8$" where it enters the dado. Carefully round the edges of the lid rails and panel on both sides of the $1/8$" expansion gap.

• The front rail of the lid starts from a $2 1/2$"-wide piece of wood. The overhanging lid lifts are carved from the rail.

• Make the trays with standard miter construction. Slightly bevel the long dividers on either end.

• Insert tray rails into the body of the box after assembly.

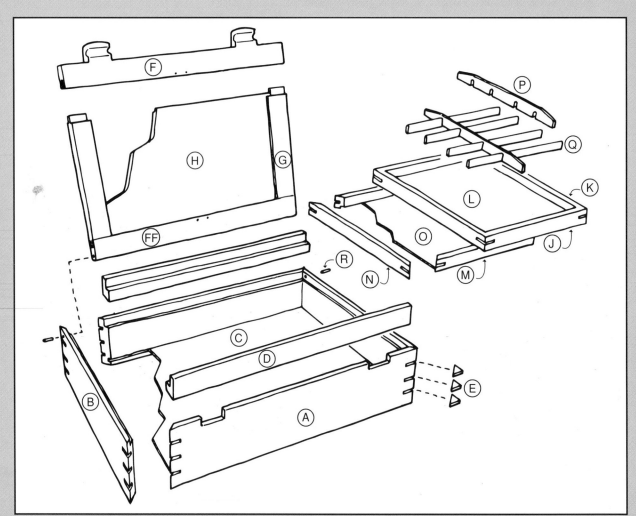

Roger Lee

Biography on page 89.

Dovetailed Chest

Photo on page 109. Exploded diagram on page 108.

This chest on a base combines Eastern and Western fiddleback maple and Hawaiian koa with bloodwood detailing. The body of the box features dovetailed construction.

• Using a $^7/_8$" bit, mill dovetail slots in two pieces of fiddleback maple, each $5^1/_4$" wide. These will become Part B (back) and Parts C and R (chest front and drawer front).

• Mill matching parts from short lengths of bloodwood. Glue in.

• Carefully cut off the excess lengths of bloodwood flush with the surface of the maple. The fiddleback pieces should be whole again, with their dovetail slots filled with bloodwood, end grain showing.

• Mill new dovetails inside the old ones, with a $^5/_8$" bit. Mill the koa sides to match. When the box is finished, the end-grain koa tails will be bordered by a perfect $^1/_8$" band of end-grain bloodwood.

• Profile the $^{13}/_{16}$"-wide koa border rails with a router. Assemble the base from a piece of $^3/_4$" plywood surrounded by the koa border rails.

• Drill the lower edges of the back and sides to receive the connecting dowels (Part E).

Dovetailed Chest

Put the sides and back together without glue. Mark the location of the dowels on the base.

• Rip one of the 5¹/₄" fiddleback pieces to produce the chest front and drawer front.

• Mill dadoes in the back for the compartment bottom. Mill dadoes in the sides for the compartment bottom and the drawer guide.

• Assemble chest front, sides, back, and compartment bottom.

• Glue in connecting dowels. Set the entire assembly on the base.

• To create the bold inlay design on the lid, start with a 2"-square block of figured maple, 10" long. With the table-saw miter fence set at a 45 degree angle, crosscut the maple block twice—once to the left and once to the right—to produce three pieces of wood, the center piece being a triangle. Insert the contrasting woods where these cuts were made. Glue the original block back together. Trim.

• The result will be the same 2" maple square, now about 12³/₄" long, with two laminate bands each consisting of two pieces of bloodwood, ¹/₈" x 2" x 3", flanking one piece of koa, ³/₄" x 2" x 3".

• Rip this block to produce eight ¹/₁₆"-thick pieces. Lay out in sequence to produce the symmetrical book-matched pattern of the lid. Trim. Glue to a ¹/₄"-thick piece of core

material. The other side of the core material should be covered with an appropriate thickness of koa veneer. Border the entire lid with a ¹/₈" bloodwood edge.

• Glue a bloodwood handle to the edge of the lid and reinforce with two dowels. Carve a notch into the chest front for

the handle to set into.

• Attach a similar handle to the drawer front.

• Prior to drawer assembly, cut ¹/₄" slots into the drawer sides to capture the drawer guides. Use a simple mortise and tenon joint to attach the drawer front to the drawer body.

Part	Description	Dimensions	Quantity
A	Side	¹/₂" x 5¹/₄" x 9¹/₂"	2
B	Back	¹/₂" x 5¹/₄" x 14³/₄"	1
C	Front (not shown)	¹/₂" x 3⁵/₈" x 14³/₄"	1
D	Base	³/₄" x 10⁵/₈" x 15³/₄"	1
E	Connecting dowel	¹/₈" x ¹/₂"	9
F	Compartment bottom	¹/₄" x 8³/₄" x 13³/₄"	1
G	Drawer guide	¹/₄" x ¹/₂" x 8¹/₂"	2
H	Compartment divider	¹/₄" x 1¹/₄" x 13³/₄"	3
H	Compartment divider	¹/₄" x 1¹/₄" x 5⁷/₈"	4
J	Lid	¹/₂" x 8¹/₂" x 13¹¹/₁₆"	1
K	Lid handle	¹/₂" x ³/₄" x 3"	1
L	Handle dowels	¹/₈" x ¹/₂"	4
M	Hinge pins	¹/₈" x ³/₄"	2
N	Tray front/back	¹/₄" x 1¹/₈" x 13⁵/₈"	2
O	Tray side	¹/₄" x 1¹/₈" x 8¹/₂"	2
P	Tray divider	¹/₄" x 1" x 8¹/₄"	3
Q	Tray bottom	¹/₈" x 8¹/₂" x 13⁵/₈"	1
R	Drawer front	¹/₂" x 1¹/₂" x 14⁵/₈"	1
S	Drawer handle	¹/₂" x ³/₄" x 3"	1
T	Drawer side	¹/₂" x 1¹/₂" x 8¹/₂"	2
U	Drawer back	¹/₂" x 1¹/₂" x 13⁵/₈"	1
V	Drawer bottom	¹/₈" x 8¹/₈" x 13¹/₈"	1
W	Drawer divider	¹/₄" x 1¹/₈" x 12³/₄"	3
X	Drawer divider	¹/₄" x 1¹/₈" x 8"	4

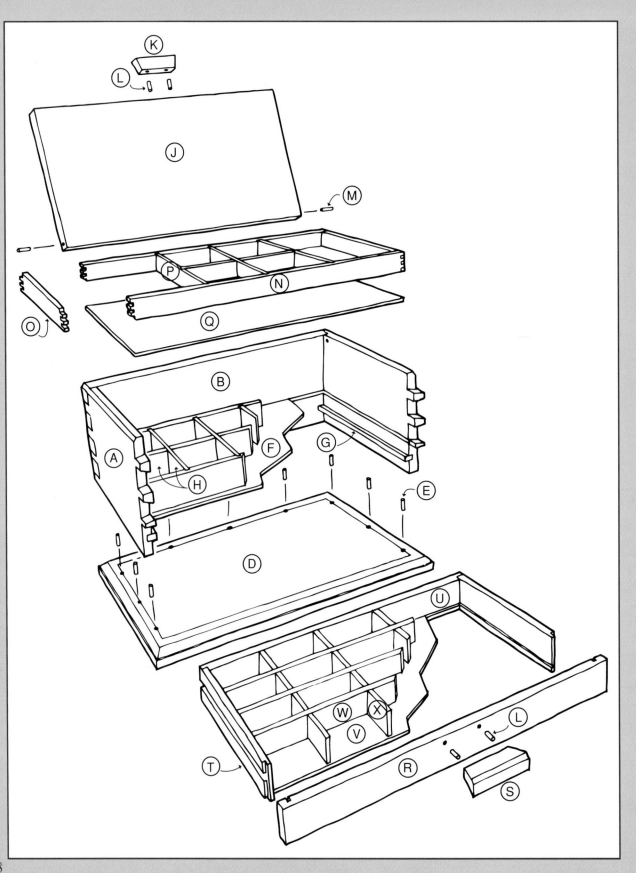

gave Ed access to the finest raw materials for the one-of-a-kind pieces he creates.

Maple Three-Drawer Chest

Photo on page 113. Exploded diagram on page 112.

This birdseye maple chests reflects the timeless beauty of traditional joinery and fine craftsmanship.

Highly figured wood such as this maple is prone to chipping and tear-out, so it is important to use only sharp carbide router bits and saw blades.

- Make the sides, bottom, and top from four pieces of maple, each carefully matched and edge-glued.
- Reduce the thickness of both the back and bottom from ⁵/₈" to ¹/₄" to allow the edges to set in a dado.
- Prior to assembly, mill ³/₈" dadoes into the sides for the drawer guides. Carefully round and polish the outer edges of these dadoes.
- Mill dovetails whose size is on a scale with the natural birdseye figure of the wood.
- Glue up the chest with two sides, top, bottom, and back.
- Use a round-over bit on a router to create the exterior radii where the sides meet the bottom and top.
- To allow the chest to lock, Ed has designed and installed a key lock, accessed from the back of the chest. Attach a cylinder lock to a sliding metal latch mechanism with three horizontal plates. When the key is turned, this latch moves up or down ³/₈", engaging or disengaging a latch block attached to the rear of each drawer (Part K).
- Mill the fronts and sides of the drawers from 1⁵/₈"- and ⁷/₈"-thick stock, respectively. Rather than attach handles and drawer guides, Ed has carved them out of the solid wood itself. Reduce the thickness of the bottom of each drawer (like the back and bottom of the chest) to set in its dado, as shown in the drawing.

Ed Wohl

Ed Wohl has always been interested in woodwork, but the seeds for the extraordinary chest shown here were planted when he was studying to be an architect. He writes, "I had the good fortune to work with an industrial designer, and that experience got me interested in making the kind of scale models architects sometimes use to show what a building project will look like. After a while, I found I enjoyed spending the day in the model-making shop much more than I did in the office."

Ed's interest led him to begin to design and build his own furniture. Ed recalls, "I had begun exhibiting larger work at local art fairs, but I found that it was slow to sell. I started making maple cutting boards, so that I would have a low-priced item people could buy when they couldn't make up their minds to buy a table or desk."

As his Wisconsin shop grew, there was another reason why cutting boards fit so well. "When I hired a helper, the first thing I trained him to do was make cutting boards. They require you to use just about every tool in the shop, and once you've mastered them, you're ready to work on furniture." They also required large quantities of birdseye maple, which

Part	Description	Dimensions	Quantity
A	Side	$\frac{5}{8}$" x $9\frac{1}{2}$" x 16"	2
B	Top	$\frac{5}{8}$" x 16" x 20"	1
C	Back	$\frac{5}{8}$" x 9" x $19\frac{1}{2}$"	1
D	Bottom	$\frac{5}{8}$" x 16" x 20"	1
E	Drawer fronts	$1\frac{5}{8}$" x $18\frac{3}{4}$" x $2\frac{1}{4}$"; $2\frac{3}{4}$"; $3\frac{1}{4}$"	3
F	Drawer sides	$\frac{7}{8}$" x $14\frac{1}{8}$" x $2\frac{1}{4}$"; $2\frac{3}{4}$"; $3\frac{1}{4}$"	6
G	Drawer backs	$\frac{1}{2}$" x $18\frac{3}{4}$" x $2\frac{1}{4}$"; $2\frac{3}{4}$"; $3\frac{1}{4}$"	3
H	Drawer bottom	$\frac{5}{8}$" x $13\frac{3}{8}$" x $18\frac{1}{4}$"	3
J	Drawer stop	$\frac{1}{2}$" x $\frac{3}{4}$" x $8\frac{3}{8}$"	2
K	Latch block	$\frac{1}{2}$" x $\frac{5}{8}$" x $1\frac{5}{8}$"	3
L	Latch	$\frac{1}{8}$" x $\frac{5}{8}$" x $6\frac{1}{2}$"	1
M	Key lock	n/a	1
N	Screw	#6 x $\frac{3}{4}$"	12
O	Drawer divider (not drawn)	$\frac{1}{8}$" x $1\frac{1}{2}$"	as req'd

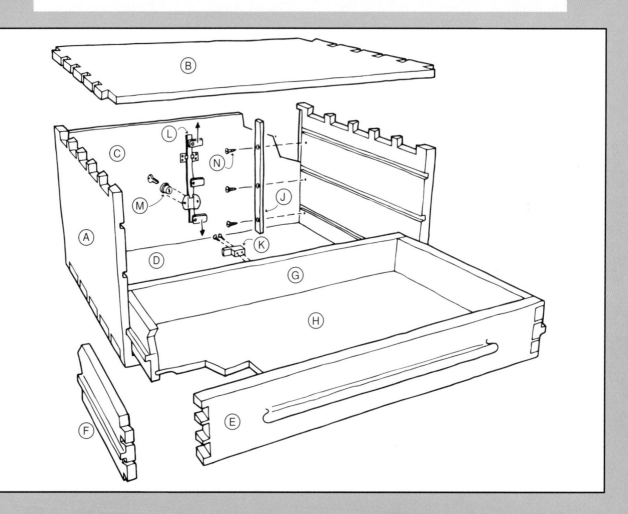

Steven Long

Photo by George Post

"For as long as I can remember, I've loved making things," writes Stephen Long from his California studio. *"I was building coasters and forts out of wood when I was eight, and later Christmas gifts for my friends. They suggested I sell my work, and that got me started showing my boxes and planters at craft shows. I never had any formal training as a woodworker, but I can learn from manuals, so I bought all the woodworking books I could afford."*

The sleekness and precision of Stephen's work have their origins in his training as an auto mechanic. He explains, "Precision has a beauty all its own. I've always liked things that are smooth and accurately machined, and that's reflected in both the fit and the feel of my boxes. In wood, you can pretty quickly make a nice enough joint. But I like to spend a horrendous amount of time and make a joint that fits to

Drawer Cabinet

a tolerance of $1/1000$ of an inch. Of course, if you sneeze, there goes your tolerance, so I don't expect to keep it for long. But making things that way is a passion, almost a need, for me.

"I began working in wood mainly because of its accessibility, but I've stayed with it because I love its warmth and tactile quality. Sometimes I wish I could find a way to work faster, but you've got to be willing to spend as much time as you need to accomplish what you've set out to do."

Drawer Cabinet

Photo on page 117. Exploded diagram on page 116.

This drawer cabinet by California box-maker Steven Long is a masterpiece of technique and design. Although the photographs and drawing give some sense of its marvellous workmanship, only close-up visual inspection can reveal the extraordinary perfection of its construction and detailing. So careful is the joinery that the delicate maple panels did not need to be glued. With slight pressure, they can be moved about in their frames.

• This drawer cabinet is created in the traditional frame and panel style.
• Mill a dado in the frames to set the panels in. Mill a keel on each edge of the maple panels.
• Detail the dark rose-

wood of both of the doors and drawer fronts with a $1/16"$ maple stripe. Carve the tiny handles from solid ebony.
• Produce subtle hints of color by thin inserts of padouk in the top edge detailing (Parts G and H) as well as in the base (Parts U and V, base details not shown in the drawing).

• Assemble the top, back, and end panels to form the body of the box, held in place by the corner rail (Part R) and end trim rail (Part Q).
• Attach the assembly to the base.
• Glue the drawer guides into dadoes milled into Part M (drawer compartment liner).

Part	Description	Dimensions	Quantity
A	Door panel	$1/4"$ x $4^3/8"$ x $4^3/8"$	2
B	Door side	$13/16"$ x $5^7/8"$ x $5^7/8"$	8
BB	Door hinge pin, brass	$1/8"$ x $3/8"$	4
C	Door & drawer handle	$1/4"$ x $1/4"$ x $7/8"$	10
D	Top panel	$1/4"$ x $6^1/8"$ x $10^3/8"$	1
E	Top front/back rail	$1/4"$ x $1"$ x $12"$	2
F	Top side rail	$1/4"$ x $1"$ x $6^3/8"$	2
G	Rail insert front/back	$1/8"$ x $1/4"$ x $12"$	2
H	Rail insert side	$1/8"$ x $1/4"$ x $7^3/4"$	2
J	Back panel	$1/4"$ x $4^1/4"$ x $9^1/2"$	1
K	Back top/bottom rail	$1/4"$ x $1"$ x $11^1/4"$	2
L	Back side rail	$1/4"$ x $1"$ x $4^1/2"$	2
M	Drawer compartment liner	$1/4"$ x $5^7/8"$ x $6^5/8"$	2
N	End panel	$1/4"$ x $4^1/2"$ x $5^1/2"$	2
O	End side rail	$1/4"$ x $1"$ x $4^1/2"$	4
P	End top/bottom rail	$1/4"$ x $1"$ x $6^3/4"$	4
Q	End trim rail	$1/4"$ x $1/2"$ x $5^7/8"$	2
R	Corner rail	$3/4"$ x $3/4"$ x $5^7/8"$	2
S	Drawer guide	$1/8"$ x $1/4"$ x $6^5/8"$	8
T	Bottom	$1/4"$ x $6^1/4"$ x $10^3/4"$	1
U	Base front/back	$7/8"$ x $7/8"$ x $12"$	2
V	Base side	$7/8"$ x $7/8"$ x $7^3/4"$	2
W	Drawer bottom	$1/8"$ x $5^7/8"$ x $10"$	4
X	Drawer front	$1/4"$ x $1^3/8"$ x $10^1/8"$	4
Y	Drawer side	$1/4"$ x $1^3/8"$ x $6^1/2"$	8
Z	Drawer back	$1/4"$ x $1^3/8"$ x $9^{11}/16"$	4
ZZ	Connecting spline	$1/8"$ x $1/4"$ x $1^3/8"$	8
AA	Spring-loaded brass catch	$1/16"$	18

Install tiny spring-loaded ball catches toward the front of each guide, as well as toward the rear of each guide slot in the four drawers and at the base of the two doors, to provide a slight pressure that will keep parts snugly in place.

- Assemble the drawers.
- Mill a ⅛" dado in each side

of the drawers to serve as a slot for the drawer guides.

- Instead of gluing the butts of the drawer backs into shallow dadoes milled into the sides, slot each part and insert a connecting spline (Part ZZ).

In the drawing, the ⅛" plywood drawer bottoms are shown fitting into dadoes. Although this is the case with the drawer front and the two sides, Steven chose to make the drawer back ⅛" narrower, and attached the bottom to the underneath edge of the back with two tiny brass screws.

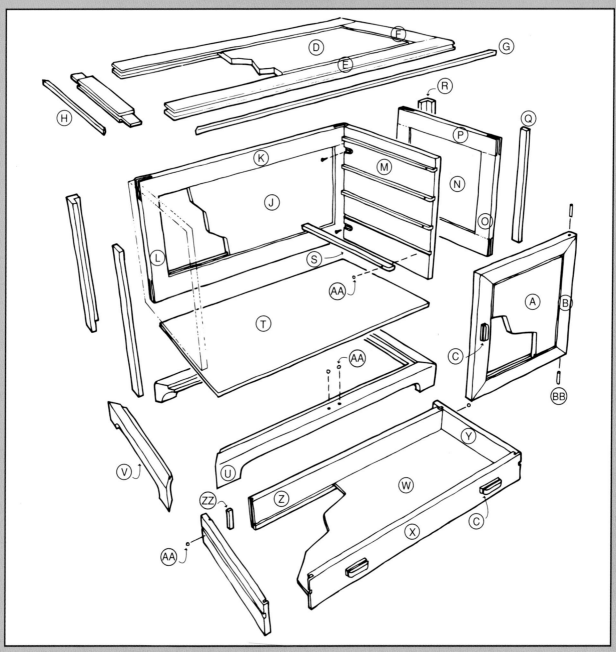

Joan Carson

"I was raised with the arts," writes Joan Carson. "Even when I was in grade school, I studied ceramics and drawing, and I learned welding as a teenager so I could do metal sculpture." Along with art, Joan was a serious student of music. One of her goals before graduating from high school was to become a concert pianist, and although she did not pursue this goal, images from music and the performing arts often appear in her work.

Her interest in social change led her to an urban studies major in college. Not long after college, she took a workshop entitled "Women in the Building Trades." She explains, "I'm a real hands-on person, and what I learned about things like carpentry, plumbing, and wiring was a welcome contrast to the academic work I was accustomed to."

After a few years as a city planner in San Francisco, Joan decided to explore woodwork as a medium for her self-expression. She served apprenticeships with furniture makers, and "read incessantly." she says, "I like to work with color and surface design in wood, however, and traditional joinery didn't give me much pleasure. What I'm doing now is a much better fit for my personality.

"Wood is definitely my canvas. It's the material that makes me feel most grounded, most like I'm home. It is rigid, yet has flexibility; it has tension, yet you can have some control. It lets me express my softness and sensuality."

"Cello"

"Cello," along with a similar piece entitled "Playing Herself," is part of a series of wall-mounted containers in which the artist interprets such themes as performance, self-expression, sensuality, and her sense of being a woman. Carved from pine, "Cello" gets its color from translucent fabric dye, followed by several coats of lacquer.

William J. Harris II

"'You'll never be able to make a living from doodling,' I remember my mother telling me," writes William J. Harris II from his studio in Georgia. "Fortunately, she encouraged me just the same." In addition to drawing and carving, William spent as much of his youth as he could exploring ways of combining whatever natural or salvaged materials he came across in his after-school walks. This early training led to the mixed-media approach that is so characteristic of his work today.

"I've always been fascinated by boxes, and I've done a series of what I call "conjure vessels." You can put whatever you want in them, but I like to think of them as containers for the owner's most personal or most cherished possessions.

"I also want to put some beauty back into our lives. As an artist, I try to be a vehicle for spirit: if you open one of my boxes in just the right way, maybe won-

derful and positive energies will emerge upon the world. One of my friends says my conjure vessels aren't designed for what can be put into them as much as for what can come out of them."

The framework of his chests is painstakingly assembled from natural hardwoods, milled and shaped using only traditional hand tools. The decorations and embellishments may include precious and semi-precious stones, seashells, found objects, or natural insects, leaves, and flowers, which William transforms into sterling silver or gold through a lost-wax casting process he taught himself.

Mixed-Media Conjure Vessel

Photos on pages 122 and 123.

The intricate frame of this chest is constructed from dozens of small pieces of ebony, purpleheart, pink ivory wood, tulipwood, and other species, each milled by hand and carefully glued in place. One face of the pyramid contains a pair of hinged doors, held open by

sliding levers. On another, a heart-shaped container swivels out, and can only be opened by removing a concealed pin. The chest is decorated with a variety of colored stones, including white and yellow jade, pearls, lapis lazuli, and garnet. To create a silver dragonfly, flowers, and other insect and plant forms, William coats the natural objects themselves with wax; a mold is then made, and the forms are exactingly reproduced in silver and other precious metals.

"Duomo" Box

Lorenzo Freccia
"Duomo" Box

Biography on page 65.

The inspiration for this architectural design came from the Piazza del Duomo, the central square in Lorenzo Freccia's hometown of Florence, Italy, where an octagonal baptistry incorporates work by a number of important artists of the Italian Renaissance. The cherry wood dome of this piece, turned on the lathe, is topped by a cupola of birdseye maple and Macassar ebony. Separated by thin strips of walnut, maple is also used for the doors and sides of the octagonal box, and the ebony reappears in the door handles, which are held in place with lacquered copper wire. The four circular cherry drawers, each lined with flocking, have walnut finger pulls.

Photo by Carol Parsons

"Self-Portrait of the Artist as a Young Man"

This sculptural container was created during an intense period of self-exploration and self-discovery, according to Michael. "At the time, I was on an inner journey, and this piece reflects some of that experience. For example, when you open the jacket, you find the bare bones—stripping down to the essentials. And the eyes turn inward, to look inside the self."

The anatomical quality of the sculpture, as well as its title, refers to a humorous story about the famous Irish writer James Joyce, author of the novel Portrait of the Artist as a Young Man, *published in 1916. "In Dublin a while ago the skull of James Joyce was put up for sale," relates Michael, who comes from a long line of Irish storytellers. "Not long afterward an entrepreneur offered another skull for sale, slightly smaller in size. It was, the owner said, Joyce's skull at a younger age."*

Standing 27" high, this lathe-turned, carved, and constructed piece, with its pivoting compartment in the base, is made of lacewood, mahogany, purpleheart, bubinga, ebony, and gold leaf.

Michael Brolly

Coming from a long line of Irish carpenters, Michael Brolly began working in wood at an early age, and made jewelry boxes, a carved chalice, and even a cradle while he was still a boy. He attended art school, where his colorful imagination and innate aesthetic ability were encouraged. "I had the good fortune to find a teacher, John Stolz, who helped me learn how to explore and develop my ideas," Michael remembers.

"My work is an evolutionary process," he explains, "facilitated by the use of the lathe as a design tool. I try to incorporate distinct personalities into my forms, whose point of departure is the circle. Since what I do becomes a living extension of me, I have a symbiotic relationship with the pieces I make, and creating that feeling of an animate personality is intrinsic to my creative process."

Both Michael's education and his career as a wood sculptor had to coexist with supporting a family, however, and he worked for twenty years in a Pennsylvania can plant. Even though he is now retired, he still is not entirely free to work full-time on sculpture. Instead, he is traveling in Ireland to do research for a book he is writing on his family, which emigrated to America during the Depression.

Eugene Watson

Photo by John Bedessem

"My father was interested in woodworking, and when I was growing up, there were always tools around," Eugene Watson remembers. "Later on, while I was in school studying to be an electronics engineer, I began to experiment with making chests and small tables. I liked the design part of working in electronics, but not the fact that it took so long to get from the drawing board to the finished component. One of the reasons I switched to woodwork was because I like something I can design and produce in a relatively short time."

Wood and electronics were brought together for Eugene during the years he played guitar in a rock band. "The original reason I bought some woodworking machinery was so I could build speakers for my band's amps and PA system. Those speakers led to chests, which led to the boxes I make today.

Ziggurat Box

"I did really well in math in school, and one of the biggest influences on the kind of work I'm doing today was trigonometry. Although I live in Chicago, I visit the Southwest whenever I can, and the look of that countryside affects me too." When asked how he made the transition from an electronics career to woodwork, Eugene said, "I just eliminated everything else in my life—band, job, school. I figured I could do it, I could make it happen, and I'm still doing that."

Ziggurat Box

Built on a 9" base, this four-level stacking box stands 7¹/₂" high. The wood is an unusually figured African bubinga, and the corner details are a laminate of bubinga and maple. These serve on the outside as handles, and on the inside as ledges on which the box above rests. Each of the four velvet-lined levels is assembled and beveled separately, so that the finished box can consist of either two, three, or four levels.

Photo by Harris From Paris

Ervin Somogyi

Many of the box-makers featured in this book have been carpenters or cabinetmakers, or made furniture or done other kinds of woodwork at some point in their careers. But only one, Ervin Somogyi of Berkeley, California, is famous as a designer and builder of guitars. In fact, he is one of the most prominent luthiers in the world.

Instruments in the guitar and lute family possess a circular sound hole, traditionally decorated with an inlaid or carved rosette. Somogyi has applied his skill to turning this decoration into an art form all its own. In his hands, the hard edge of a steel cutting tool acquires the fluidity of a painter's brushstroke.

"To make one of these carvings, I start with a thin piece of guitar-top wood, such as cedar or spruce. Soft woods like these take a clean cut without too much pressure," he says. With the help of his assistant, Kalia Kliban, he uses surgical scalpels for most of the cuts, but it is persistence and elbow grease that really get the job done. A single panel may contain as many as 3,000 separate cut lines, each requiring up to fifteen individual cutting strokes.

"There's no room to go very far with a rosette design on an actual instrument, so I've turned to boxes—and now this wall chest—to give me the chance to explore larger and more intricate forms."

Wall-Mounted Chest

This ash cabinet opens to reveal three adjustable-height velvet-lined tray shelves. On the back of the door, Ervin has used a part from his other life as an instrument maker: one of his hand-carved guitar bridges, with its six ebony pegs, serves to hold necklaces or chains. The other non-ash detail is a slim handle on the lower right side of the door, made from pernambuco, a wood used for violin bows.

The exterior of the door is a $1/16$" thin sheet of Alaskan yellow cedar. There are over three hundred lines in its wonderfully tight grain, meaning that the tree had been growing at least since the year 1690. Ervin's skill in carving, developed over years of making lute rosettes, has given the swimming carp an extraordinary lifelike feel. To reinforce the cedar during carving, the area under the design is lined with parchment. A surgical scalpel is used for the hundreds of individual cuts that make up the design, and the finished panel is mounted above a recessed background of black velvet.

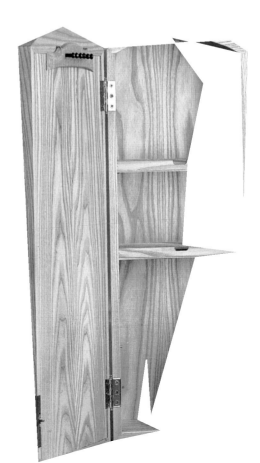

Joel Gelfand

Biography on page 18.

Key-Lock Chest

This chest is made of dovetailed bubinga, with rosewood slipfeathers in the base and oak burl doors. The drawer fronts are cherry. Plugs fashioned from tagua nut cover the screws that attach the hinges to the chest. The five drawers ride on rails dadoed in the sides of the chest. Each drawer is lined with velvet. The lock mechanism is based on a Moroccan design, and is opened by gentle pressure from the brass-pinned key.

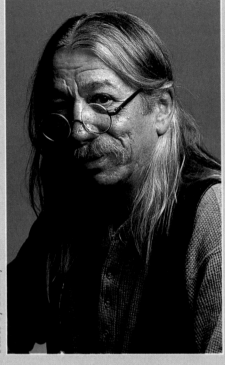

Bill McDowell

"I started a production shop with a partner about twenty years ago," Bill McDowell writes, "and we were quite successful. 'Wood Goods,' as we called our enterprise, ran a fairly large shop, with several full-time employees, and forty to fifty galleries carried our work nationwide. After a while, though, it was time for me to go off in my own direction."

That direction turned out to include furniture and a series of boxes and clocks that Bill calls "Art Tekno-Deco." In this continually evolving, five-year progression, Bill explores his fascination with juxtaposing the organic and the manufactured, the mechanical and the sensual, the practical and the sublime.

"These designs are very distinctive, and it's interesting how people respond to them. My latch mechanism, for example, seems to evoke images from science fiction, particularly the Starship Enterprise. I'm not really sure myself where the inspiration comes from, so I guess anyone's interpretation is both a little bit right and a little bit wrong."

Like many box-makers, Bill is a graduate of seventh-grade woodshop, who went on to study industrial and product design in college. "In my boxes I emphasize crisp lines, and linear, almost metallic forms. When it comes to furniture, though, I go out of my way to incorporate the wood's natural splits, gnarls, and rotten spots. That's why wood is my medium: it's the only material where high-tech and organic are equally at home."

Gold Chain Box

Bill McDowell's signature latch mechanism also appears on this box, made of walnut, wenge, purpleheart, fiddleback maple, and cherry. It is opened by placing the thumb on the group of three purpleheart horizontals at the top right of the box, and the second finger on the end of the horizontal wenge dowel, and squeezing. This compresses a concealed spring and allows the wenge latch to disengage.

This box has a cushioned compartment for rings, but its primary purpose is to hold narrow necklaces and chains. When placed on the wenge hooks on the inside of the lid, their lengths fall neatly into the slotted compartments in the box bottom, thus preventing tangling. When this box is placed on a dressing table, the slightly more than half-circle mirror is just at eye level.

Bill McDowell

Biography on page 135.

Ring Box

Bill McDowell's boxes are marvels of mechanism and intricacy, all in the service of safekeeping that which is precious. This wenge, padouk, koa, and maple ring box is opened by placing the thumb on the group of three padouk horizontals at the top of the box, and the second finger at the rear of the horizontal wenge dowel, and then squeezing. This compresses a concealed spring and allows the wood latch to disengage. The lid rocks back on its invisible pin hinge, revealing a small space for precious object number one. At the same time, the front of the box is freed to fall open, drawbridge style, and the delicate padouk compartment within contains a velvet-lined cushion assembly for six rings.

Photo by David Ashcraft

Christopher Cantwell

It is unusual for a woodworker to work at a professional level while still in high school, but Christopher Cantwell sold his first piece of furniture, an ash dining table, when he was only fifteen. Three years before that, he won the Young Masters competition at the Central California Art League.

Mostly self-taught, Christopher educated himself by reading books and articles on woodworking, and by studying every wooden object he could find to see how it was made. After a career detour that included construction work, cabinetmaking, guitar building, and becoming a world-class rock climber, Christopher returned full-time to his first love.

Most of his work includes one-of-a-kind elements that harmonize with the character of the many different species of wood he uses. "I like to design with the actual pieces of wood," Christopher says. "Things like the shape of a box leg, or how to place inlays within the flow of the grain—these create a dialogue between me and the wood."

His current work is divided among boxes, functional mirror chests like the one featured here, and nonfunctional wall pieces. All are well represented in major collections, including the White House, and Christopher and his unique style are frequently the subject of newspaper and magazine articles.

Mirrored Wall Chest

Christopher Cantwell has developed a style that combines classical cabinetry with intricate, flowing inlays using a wide variety of woods. The body of this wall-mounted mirror cabinet is made from a piece of figured granadilla that includes a band of rich cream-colored sapwood. The door and drawer fronts are cocobolo. They and the mirror are bordered with ziricote.

The remarkable inlay that meanders over the surfaces, which Christopher refers to as his "waterfall" style, consists of a stream of small irregularly shaped sections of colorful hardwoods, including koa, ebony, kingwood, zebra, satinwood, purpleheart, chacticote, pink ivory, snakewood, maple, and even black oak, which Christopher salvaged from a tree in his backyard. These handmade $1/8$"-thick inlays are painstakingly assembled across the doors and drawer fronts. After gluing them down, Christopher fills the minute voids between them with a mixture of ebony dust and glue.

Photo by Ray Upchurch

Gregory Williams

It was in 1974, while living near Bear Wallow, Kentucky, that Greg Williams realized he had a greater affinity for woodworking than for the chemical engineering he had been studying in school. Not long afterward, an elderly blues guitar player agreed to sell Greg a set of woodworking tools, and that settled the matter.

Greg named his woodworking business "Zeke Towne Woodworks" after a historic Kentuckian. A short series of visits to New York City during the 1980s, however, had the greatest impact on the distinctive shapes of his jewelry boxes. He explains, "I took a night

school course in design that led me to books on Mayan architecture and Art Deco. After I came back home, any chunk of wood I picked up to work on just seemed to go that Mayan Deco way.

"Not long afterward, an old pallet factory in my neighborhood closed down. One thing led to another, and I ended up owning thousands of board feet of lumber, all native Appalachian species, like butternut, hickory, walnut, and cherry. I don't have to go to the lumberyard anymore—I am the lumberyard." Thanks to his engineering background, Greg has an uncanny ability to combine these woods into unusual constructions and elaborate shapes.

Pyramid Box

Photo on page 142.

Using native Appalachian species, like walnut, hickory, butternut, oak, and cherry, Greg Williams has designed a series of pyramid boxes, each with a unique combination of features. Three pull-out drawers stand at the front of this temple-like version, which is approximately 16" square at the base. Above them are additional swing-out drawers, topped by a single compartment at the apex of the pyramid.

Metric Equivalency

mm-millimeters cm-centimeters
inches to millimeters and centimeters

inches	mm	cm	inches	cm	inches	cm
⅛	3	0.3	9	22.9	30	76.2
¼	6	0.6	10	25.4	31	78.7
½	13	1.3	12	30.5	33	83.8
⅝	16	1.6	13	33.0	34	86.4
¾	19	1.9	14	35.6	35	88.9
⅞	22	2.2	15	38.1	36	91.4
1	25	2.5	16	40.6	37	94.0
1¼	32	3.2	17	43.2	38	96.5
1½	38	3.8	18	45.7	39	99.1
1¾	44	4.4	19	48.3	40	101.6
2	51	5.1	20	50.8	41	104.1
2½	64	6.4	21	53.3	42	106.7
3	76	7.6	22	55.9	43	109.2
3½	89	8.9	23	58.4	44	111.8
4	102	10.2	24	61.0	45	114.3
4½	114	11.4	25	63.5	46	116.8
5	127	12.7	26	66.0	47	119.4
6	152	15.2	27	68.6	48	121.9
7	178	17.8	28	71.1	49	124.5
8	203	20.3	29	73.7	50	127.0

yards to meters

yards	meters	yards	meters	yards	meters	yards	meters	yards	meters
⅛	0.11	2⅛	1.94	4⅛	3.77	6⅛	5.60	8⅛	7.43
¼	0.23	2¼	2.06	4¼	3.89	6¼	5.72	8¼	7.54
⅜	0.34	2⅜	2.17	4⅜	4.00	6⅜	5.83	8⅜	7.66
½	0.46	2½	2.29	4½	4.11	6½	5.94	8½	7.77
⅝	0.57	2⅝	2.40	4⅝	4.23	6⅝	6.06	8⅝	7.89
¾	0.69	2¾	2.51	4¾	4.34	6¾	6.17	8¾	8.00
⅞	0.80	2⅞	2.63	4⅞	4.46	6⅞	6.29	8⅞	8.12
1	0.91	3	2.74	5	4.57	7	6.40	9	8.23
1⅛	1.03	3⅛	2.86	5⅛	4.69	7⅛	6.52	9⅛	8.34
1¼	1.14	3¼	2.97	5¼	4.80	7¼	6.63	9¼	8.46
1⅜	1.26	3⅜	3.09	5⅜	4.91	7⅜	6.74	9⅜	8.57
1½	1.37	3½	3.20	5½	5.03	7½	6.86	9½	8.69
1⅝	1.49	3⅝	3.31	5⅝	5.14	7⅝	6.97	9⅝	8.80
1¾	1.60	3¾	3.43	5¾	5.26	7¾	7.09	9¾	8.92
1⅞	1.71	3⅞	3.54	5⅞	5.37	7⅞	7.20	9⅞	9.03
2	1.83	4	3.66	6	5.49	8	7.32	10	9.14

Index